CREATIVE PROBLEM-SOLVING AND DECISION-MAKING

How to get off the fence and make decisions

Roberta Cava

Published by Cava Consulting

cavaconsulting@ozemail.com.au

www.dealingwithdifficultpeople.info

Cava, Roberta

Creative Problem-Solving and Decision-Making

How to get off the fence and make decisions

National Library of Australia
Cataloguing-in-publication data:

ISBN 9780994436597

BOOKS BY ROBERTA CAVA

All can be purchased from Amazon Books

Non-Fiction

Dealing with Difficult People

(International best-seller since 1990 with 24 publishers – in
18 languages in over 100 countries)
Kein Problem mit Schwierigen Menschen (German)
Tratando con Gente Difícil (Spanish)
Traiter avec des personnes difficiles (French)
Comunicareaea cu oameni dificili (Romanian)

Dealing with Difficult Situations – at Work and at Home
Tratando con Situationes Dificiles (Spanish)

Dealing with Difficult Spouses and Children
Tratando con Cónyuges y Niños Difíciles

Dealing with Difficult Relatives and In-Laws
Tratando con parientes difíciles y en leyes

Dealing with School Bullying
Tratando con la Intimidación en la Escouela (Spanish)

Dealing with Workplace Bullying
Tratando con Intimidación en el lugar de trabajo

Keeping Our Children Safe
Mantenera Nuestros Hijos Seguros (Spanish)

Dealing with Domestic Violence and Child Abuse
Retirement Village Bullies
Just say no
What am I going to do with the rest of my life?
Interpersonal Communication at Work
Change? Not me!
Creative Problem-Solving & Decision-Making
Customer Service that Works
Teambuilding
How Women can advance in business

Before Tying the Knot – Questions couples must ask each
other before they marry!
Survival Skills for Supervisors and Managers
Human Resources at its Best!
Human Resources Policies and Procedures - Australia
Employee Handbook
Easy Come – Hard to go – The Art of Hiring, Disciplining
and Firing Employees
Time and Stress – Today's silent killers
Take Command of your Future – Make things Happen!
The Presenter
Belly Laughs for All! – Volumes 1 to 8
Australian Trivia volumes 1, 2 and 3
Trivia and More – Volumes 1, 2, 3, 4 and 5
Australian Sports Trivia
Wisdom of the World! The happy, sad & wise things in life!
Covid19 - 200 Days – Facts and Fun
Covid 19 - 200-400 Days – Facts and Fun
Covid 19 - 400-600 Days – Facts and Fun
Covid 19 - 600-800 Days – Facts and Fun
Covid 19 - 800-1,000 Days – Facts and Fun

Fiction

I can do it! The sky's the limit!
Twists and Turns
Treacherous Livelihoods
Life Gets Complicated
Life Goes On
Life Gets Better

That Something Special

CREATIVE PROBLEM-SOLVING
AND DECISION-MAKING

How to get off the fence and make decisions

Table of Contents

Don't value or respect others' opinions
Don't give recognition for a job well done
Don't back up their staff when dealing with
    customer complaints
Don't provide adequate up-to-date job descript-
    tions with key performance indicators
Hire the wrong staff
    Reference checking
Don't provide the necessary training
Conduct performance appraisals on staff without
    a proper job description
Use the same leadership style on all members
    Theory X and Theory Y
Have one set of company rules for staff
    – another for themselves
Don't provide policies and procedures for
    employees
Have poor work ethic
Do nothing to improve the employee's interest
    in their jobs
Are not available when staff need their help
Won't listen to their staff's suggestions about
    better ways to complete tasks
Have a negative *"That will never work"* attitude
Are perfectionists
Are workaholics
Upper management have not given supervisor
    full responsibility to perform their duties
Use authoritarian management style
Supervisor ignores issues when staff member's
    behaviour requires correction
Don't step in to resolve personality conflicts
    between staff
Show favouritism towards *"Pet employees."*
Poor role models
Don't know how to manage their time
Allow nepotism
Don't keep promises

Too immature for supervisory role
Bring personal problems into the workplace
Promoted too soon

Learning a new skill
Retention of information
Training of others
Training vs Development
Career development
Training procedure
Tangible/intangible behaviour
Setting objectives
Identifying costs of training
Methods of instruction
Preparing to present a seminar/workshop
Group vs individual activities
Technical vs life skills
Theoretical/practical training
Bridging
Timing of training segments
Use of training aids
Re-enforcement of training'
How to keep participants motivated
Instructor's apparel
Presentation skills
Methods I use

Career changes
Help yourself to a mid-career change
Making mid-life career changes
Obstacles holding you back from making a
    career change
    Fear of disapproval from others
    Fear of being *"locked in"*

INTRODUCTION

There are many times every day that supervisors/managers face problems or must make decisions – some of them very serious ones. If you find yourself holding off making decisions, you might find that it keeps you from progressing up the ladder in your corporation. Procrastination is one of the things that companies say keeps them from promoting good employees; employees who could be very good managers or executives of a company except for the flaw that they were poor problem-solvers or were reluctant to making decisions.

Don't let this be the one quality that holds you back from advancing in business or even finding happiness by making the right decisions in your personal life. If you are in a rut within either phase of your life, you should find this information helpful to assist you in becoming the person you could be.

This book discusses many areas where supervisors/ managers must problem-solve – some that can be highly stressful or emotional.

CHAPTER 1

PROBLEM SOLVING

We're constantly using the word *"problem"* in our daily lives. You would think that our everyday lives were nothing but problems. There are problems at work, with children, with money, car problems, health problems and even love problems. The list goes on and on.

A problem occurs if:

"A need, a wish, a desire, an objective or question appears, and we don't know the series of actions required to fill the void."

To solve a problem, the person must be clear about the following:

The actual situation:

The Gap: (The Problem):

The Ideal Situation.

When they have a problem most people dive right in and try to solve their problem without thinking it through. Unfortunately, most just end up spinning their wheels, because they haven't taken the time to establish that they're tackling the right problem and have taken the necessary time to think things through.

Others whine and complain to others but do nothing to solve their problems.

Are you a *"fence sitter?"* (Someone who has a terrible time making decisions. This person usually involves several others before even attempting to decide). Others just keep putting it off.

Is this you? Let's try to correct that.

How do you solve complex problems?

1. Outline on paper the steps you normally go through when solving complex problems. It might help to think of a recent problem you've had. (5 minutes)

2. Do you involve others?

3. Do you write down your problems?

4. Have any set way of solving personal problems?

Don't undertake the responsibility of solving any problem unless you're willing to make the commitment to solving it. There are criteria you should consider when defining problems:

Three criteria required for defining problems:

1. Specific Problem Definition:

Specific Problem: Must be detailed, quantitative and measurable.

General Problem: Is vague, difficult to measure.

Sample Situation - How to raise production levels:

This problem definition is too large and too general. Try breaking it down into smaller, more specific components.

Revised Example: How to motivate John smith so his work output improves by 20 per cent before April 5, 20__.

Specific Problem: i.e.: How to improve my health.

The difficulty with this statement is that not only is it too general, but it lacks any measurable commitment on the part of the person trying to solve it.

Revised Example: How to lose 10 pounds.

2. Ownership of the Problem:

To establish ownership, you must ask yourself:

a. Is this problem mine or someone else's? (In the first case it *is* this person's problem, because he's a supervisor, therefore he's ultimately responsible for the productivity of his staff).

b. Do I have the power and authority to put the solution into practice? Yes, he does. He's the employee's supervisor.

3. Personal Commitment to Solving the Problem:

The person needs to be willing to put forth the effort necessary to solve their problem.

Note: each problem statement must satisfy the above three criteria.

Next, define whether your problem is:

A short-term problem: 1 day, one month?

A long-term problem: More than one month?

If problems are long term, the incentive to solve them is harder. We put these kinds of problems on the *"back burner"* and they often aren't solved.

A tangible problem: Something you can see, such as an object.

An intangible problem: Something you can't see, such as attitudes, feelings or behaviour.

Intangible problems are the hardest to solve. Tangible problems involve something you can see and feel, whereas intangible problems involve feelings, attitudes and behaviour.

Sample problem:

Here's a short-term problem. See how you think you would solve it:

You're leaving for work and find that your car will start, but it stalls and won't keep running properly.

The Specific Problem: (What is it?)

a)   To get my car started and running or

b)   To get to work on time?

Ownership of the problem: (Who owns this problem? Do I own this problem? Yes!)

a) I need a method or way of keeping my car's engine running once it starts or

b) I need to find a way to get to work on time (other than in my car).

Personal commitment to solving the problem: Am I willing to make the effort to solve this problem?

a) I'm looking for ways to keep my car's engine running for a minimum of thirty minutes or

b) I'm looking for an alternative form of transportation to get me to work by 9:00 am or

c) I think I'll go back to bed (gives up - no commitment to solving the problem).

Dealing with your own problems:

To practice the process, identify a simple problem you've been wrestling with lately. When you've written it down, define whether it's specific enough (detailed, quantitative, precise, measurable) or was it too general (broad, vague, difficult to measure)

Was it a tangible problem (something you can see) or was it intangible (something you can't see)? As you've probably guessed, intangible problems are harder to solve and solutions are much harder to evaluate.

Was your problem a short or long-term problem?

Here' a sample method to work through your problem. It is a cut-down version of one problem solving system I found that had twenty-seven steps to it. Who has time for twenty-seven steps! This one has eleven and two of them are for evaluation purposes only.

It's an aide to keep you from wasting valuable time. Unfortunately, most people waste time, energy and effort by trying to solve the wrong problem. This guide will help you determine the *real* problem:

Problem-solving and decision-making guide

(It's best to do this guide in pencil, because you'll probably change your mind on what really is the problem half way through the process).

Step 1: The factual situation

Step 2: The ideal situation

Step 3: The problem (or cause of the gap)

Step 4: List the symptoms of the problem

What's happening and why.

Where it's happening and why.

When it occurs and why.

Who's involved and why.

How it happens and why.

Did you find that after completing steps 1-4 that you revised your problem? If so, repeat steps 1 to 4 again. You may even revise the problem twice, but at least you will be tackling the *real* problem. Be sure to circle your actual problem because that will have a bearing on the rest of the problem-solving process.

Now look at Step 5 that defines the driving and restraining forces. This is a step many people miss but can be very important in the problem-solving process. Once you have done that, go on to the rest of the steps in this process.

Step 5: List the Driving and Restraining forces

Driving Forces: (The benefits of solving the problem).

These are forces that are in favour of your problem being solved. They are the benefits that will result when you solve the problem.

Restraining Forces: (Obstacles you must overcome to solve the problem).

These are forces that are against your problem being solved. They are the things that stand in the way of getting your problem solved.

Step 6: Identify how you will overcome the obstacles you've identified.

Step 7: List all the possible solutions to your problem - (brainstorm):

Step 8: Choose the best solution:

Step 9: Formulate an Action Plan:

    Steps or Actions:
    Date or time limit:
    People to Involve:
    Resources required:

Step 10: Implement your action plan

Step 11: Evaluate the success of your action plan

Here are several definitions that will help you understand the above method:

Driving Forces: Make a list of these

Restraining Forces: Make a list of these

Because this method is putting information down on paper, you might save yourself the physical effort of solving the problem. By doing it on paper first, you might find that the obstacles in your way of solving the problem may be so overwhelming that you decide not to spend the effort on trying to solve it.

Brainstorming:

I've watched supervisors take three days to come up with a solution when brainstorming with the affected staff could have come up with a solution in fifteen minutes. It's a tool that far too few supervisors use.

For example: *"We seem to be having more than our usual share of customer complaints. I'm open to suggestions on how you think we can solve this problem and who should handle customer complaints in the future."* The group would then brainstorm until they came up with viable solutions.

Another advantage of getting your staff involved in problem-solving (especially when it involves changing how something is done) is that if they are in on making the decision - they're less likely to balk at the change.

Brainstorming is the process of generating ideas or creating solutions in either individual or group situations where the climate is free-wheeling and open. It is an ideal process all supervisors should use with their staff. Instead of spending three days mulling over a problem, get your staff involved. They'll likely come up with a solution in fifteen to twenty minutes (and probably a better one as well). Here's how you do this:

1. **Limit the topic to a single question**, e.g., how to deal with absenteeism.

2. **Encourage idea quantity**. At this point, don't consider quality of ideas. What you're seeking are as many ideas and suggestions as possible.

3. **Encourage wild thinking** - offer any idea (no matter how questionable). Encourage the group to build on one another's ideas, altering, expanding and modifying them. Again, the purpose here is to get ideas - not to pass judgment on them.

4. **Discourage critical judgement and evaluation**. Don't allow anyone to say, *"That won't work because..."* during a brainstorming session. You're looking for ways of getting ideas, not trying to suppress them. Someone's idea (that really won't work) might just be the thing that triggers someone else to think of one that *will* work.

For example: In one of my sessions where I had explained this concept, the class received the following problem:

The Problem: My car is stuck in mud, what should I do?

Everyone gave suggestions such as:

Push the car.

Pull the car.

9

Call a tow truck.

Call spouse.

Flag down another car.

In brainstorming it's a good idea to slip in something funny during the brainstorming. Examples of some of the funny suggestions were:

Bury my car.

Wait until the mud dries.

Sell my car.

Show a little leg (females).

Blow up my car.

The last one gave the mental picture of a car flying up in the air and coming down in pieces. This prompted the suggestion:

Jack up the car and carefully push it to the side off the jack which should get it out of the rut.

This bizarre suggestion triggered an excellent solution that I've used the idea to get my car out of mud one day.

5. **Avoid side discussion and issues**. During the actual brainstorming (which is of very short duration) don't allow side discussions. Ask all members of the group to concentrate their energies towards coming up with additional ideas.

6. **Don't allow outside observers.** Everyone in the room must participate. It may be wise to require everyone to offer at least two suggestions during the session.

7. **Have an idea or two in the back of your head** to provide a trigger to get the session moving. Once it begins, ideas come fast and furious.

One member of the group should **take notes,** recording the ideas as fast as they're offered. It's a good idea to have the suggestions listed on a flip chart or white board where everyone can see them. Previous ideas provide food for thought and lead to further ideas.

The brainstorming session itself **should not last** less than five minutes or more than fifteen. Shorter time doesn't allow enough good ideas to surface and after fifteen minutes, most of ideas become clearly impractical.

Brainstorming encourages synergy. One person may only come up with two ideas; two people might come up with two more, but when you have people bouncing ideas off each other they often come up with solutions that none of them would have contemplated on their own. This is what creative problem solving is all about.

One time a manager could not attend a meeting, so he sent his secretary instead.

Brainstorming was a tool devised to assist in creative problem solving. Initially, most of those who used the technique were men. This technique proved moderately successful until a manager couldn't make it to a meeting, so sent his secretary to take notes for him. Since everyone had to participate, she contributed as well. The managers couldn't believe the outcome - she came up with two of the four workable suggestions. They couldn't understand why her answers were better than those of professionals who understood all aspects of the problem.

At the next meeting, they tried an experiment. All the managers brought their secretaries to the meeting. Most of the ideas again came from the women! The women didn't censor their own ideas as critically as the men. Before speaking, most men generally examined their ideas to see if they are *"good enough"* before submitting them to the group. Some did this out of a fear of looking silly and some because they couldn't turn off the self-censoring mechanism that told them, *"That won't work."*

In this case, the women were instructed to let ideas flow unrestricted - so they did. They suggested any idea they could think of. It didn't matter whether it was a good idea, because they knew their suggestions would be evaluated after the brainstorming session.

If the men had practiced listening to their *"gut reactions"* the way the women listened to their *"intuitions"* they wouldn't have had this problem. Many businesses now make sure half the participants in creative problem-solving sessions are women.

Let your *"little kid"* out and allow your creative juices to flow. You'll be surprised how effective it is - not only thinking up advertising campaigns or marketing a product - but in finding creative solutions to difficult problems. It will allow you to take something that is average and make it superior.

Personal problem solving

Here's another example of problem-solving, but this time involving your personal life:

Suppose your physician has told you that you are ten kg overweight and that you *must* go on a diet?

What are the driving forces (benefits when problem is solved) for you to lose weight?

Look better

Feel better

Be healthier

Better athletic ability

Higher self-esteem

Less shortness of breath

Less strain on my heart

Be less tired

Could buy a new wardrobe

What are the restraining forces (obstacles to solving the problem) that will keep you from losing weight?

I will need to change eating habits

Lack of willpower

Must give up favourite foods

Clothing would need to be altered or look at extra expense for a new wardrobe

Must exercise more

My friends all eat high calorie foods

I must cook for my family as well as my self

I like to eat!

Use brainstorming for step 6 and 7.

Step 6 - What will you do to overcome the obstacles you identified in Step 5?

In the case of the overweight person, to overcome restraining forces:

I will need to change my eating habits.

    I need to talk to dietician for help

I lack willpower.

    I should join weight watchers

I must give up favourite foods.

    I need to find foods I like

Clothing would need to be altered or I might have an extra expense for a new wardrobe.

    I would need to have a garage sale to earn money so I can buy or alter wardrobe

Must exercise more.

    Should consider exercising with a friend

My friends all eat high calorie foods.

    When they're having their gooey cinnamon buns at coffee-break - go for a walk around the block and eat an apple.

I must cook for my family.

    They might be overweight too. Encourage them to eat better foods too.

I like to eat!

Find new low-calorie snacks you enjoy.

Do you use brainstorming in your personal or business life? Consider an example of where you could be using the brainstorming technique but aren't.

Try Brainstorming

Find a simple problem and discuss the solution of it with another person. Then discuss it with more than one person.

Did you find that someone else's idea triggered a good one in you?

Did you follow the rules of brainstorming?

Were there any side conversations?

Did you revise your problem statement after completing Step 4?

Do you feel you can now solve your problem?

How effective was the step on driving/restraining forces?

Were any good ideas obtained from brainstorming with another person? Did you find more ideas than you would normally have come up with without brainstorming?

Any spin-off problems identified?

Tackling the wrong problem

I remember a time where a company had hired me to do a motivational seminar for their staff. They had a high turnover of staff and thought they required motivation to enjoy their jobs better. I conducted the one-day session which was well received by the participants. However, when I followed-up a while later, found that the turnover rate was still as high as before.

I asked the Human Resources person whether they had conducted exit interviews for the employees who had left. They had not done so. I asked whether I could conduct one on the employees who had left in the past two months and was given the go-ahead. In all cases, their reason for leaving was because of the terrible supervisor they all had reported to.

So, the company did not investigate to see what was causing the low morale and overlooked the real reason for the turnover (a bad boss). They tackled the 'real' problem and the turnover stopped immediately.

Here's an example of how a person used the Problem Solving and Decision-making Guide:

Using the Problem-solving and decision-making guide

Step 1: The factual situation

I'm having trouble getting along with my boss

Step 2: The ideal situation

I'd like to get along with my boss.

Step 3: The problem (or cause of the gap)

He's inconsistent - changes his mind, so I don't know what he expects of me.

Step 4: List the symptoms of the problem

What's happening and why:

I'm frustrated because I can't do a good job.

Where it's happening and why:

At the office - my boss is inconsistent and often changes his mind.

When it occurs and why:

When he gives me assignments, he doesn't seem sure of what he's to do; therefore, he has trouble delegating assignments to me.

Who's involved and why:

My boss and his boss (his boss starts the problem). Neither of them seems to be clear on what they want me to do.

How it happens and why:

Lack of clear directives from my boss.

Note: After answering these questions, it's clear that I've identified the *"real"* problem (not just the perceived one) so I must go through the process again:

Revised Problem:

Step 1: The factual situation:

I don't know what my boss expects of me.

Step 2: The Ideal Situation:

To know what my boss expects of me.

Step 3: The problem (or cause of the gap):

Lack of clear directives from my boss.

Step 4: (Complete this step again to confirm that your problem is the real problem.)

Step 5: List the driving and restraining forces

Driving forces:

I'll know what I'm supposed to do.

I can meet boss's needs.

I can do a better job.

I can risk-take more.

I'll learn more.

Restraining Forces:

I need communication skills.

Could cause spin-off problems with boss if not done correctly.

Could lose face with boss.

Need the nerve to do it.

Preparation time to do it.

Step 6: Identify how you will overcome the obstacles you've identified.

Read some books on how to communicate better.

Rehearse what I am going to say, so I feel comfortable doing so.

Find a suitable time for both me and my boss to discuss this issue.

Step 7: List all possible solutions - (Brainstorm):

Ask for written directions from my boss.

Write boss's verbal directions down and confirm with him.

Explain my frustrations to my boss and ask for his help.

Find another job.

Try to organise my boss.

Ask for more information when project explained.

Quit.

Tell my boss what I think of his disorganisation.

Step 8: Choose the best solution

Explain my frustrations to my boss and ask for his help.

Step 9: Formulate an action plan

Steps or actions: Make a list of my frustrations and possible solutions.
Date or Time Limit: Tonight.
People to Involve: Me.
Resources Required: Pen and paper, ideas, time

Steps or actions: Ask for a meeting with my boss.
Date or Time Limit: Tomorrow.
People to Involve: Me, my boss.
Resources Required: Courage, my prepared list

Step 10: Implement your action plan

Meeting held (date).

Step 11: Evaluate the success of your action plan

*Much improved relations with my boss. He's as frustrated as I am at **his** lack of direction from **his** boss. Together we're formulating a plan initially to help him, then me.*

Note: There's now a new problem!

If you haven't worked out a problem on paper before, try this method with a simple problem. If you don't go through it, you won't be able to clarify in your mind that it really works. Otherwise, it's possible that you'll spend far too much energy trying to solve the wrong problem.

It also gives you the opportunity of *"walking through"* the problem, without physically doing it. You'll be able to identify restraining forces that might get in the way of solving your problem. After identifying these restraining forces, you may decide that the time, energy and effort you'd need to spend, wouldn't be worth the results. You'll have saved yourself considerable grief by not actually trying to solve it (except on paper).

For other problems, you may find that you can get allies to help you. These are people who would be favourably affected if you solved the problem. Or you may decide that the problem isn't so earth-shattering after all. It helps to stop procrastination and keeps you moving forward towards finding solutions to problems.

What do you do when you're faced with others who refuse to make decisions and instead, you'd class them as:

Whiners, Complainers and Bellyachers:

They're chronic gripers who grumble about everything - publicly and privately. They're cry babies who voice protracted protests over the unimportant. Driven by childish insecurity, they complain when everything's going well. They love to exaggerate unfair workloads, tardy reports, broken rules - whatever they can blame on somebody else. Although their work is good, they usually don't sound off about legitimate problems. When whiners warn you of trouble ahead, their intent is to establish an excuse in advance of a feared failure. To overcome:

1. *When they start griping, obtain their permission to let you help them find solutions to their problems. If they*

don't allow you to help, go to step seven. If they accept your help - proceed to step two.

2. *Have them write down the <u>specific</u> problem. (This might take some time to determine.)*

3. *Ask them to write down all the possible solutions to the problem. You can suggest others.*

4. *Have them identify the benefits/disadvantages (pros and cons) of each solution. Using a point system might help. For instance, possibly the cost of solving the problem might be crucial.*

5. *Have THEM choose the best solution. (They might say, "What do you think I should do?" Don't take the bait - because if you suggest the best solution - and it doesn't work - they'll be the first to say, "I told you it wouldn't work!")*

6. *Have them write the steps they will take to achieve the solution (giving deadlines).*

7. *Refuse to talk about the topic in the future.*

Note: This is an ideal tactic to use if *you're* the one who has become a whiner, complainer and bellyacher yourself (leaving out #7). It is also a simple method you can use if you must make complicated decisions.

CHAPTER TWO

PLANNING FOR PROBLEM-SOLVING

Would you describe yourself as organised?

Do you plan your day on paper?

Somehow, when you plan on paper, it takes on more importance, and you're likely to follow-through with your plan. Planning eliminates guesswork from your job. Whether you build a plan quickly in your head, or develop it slowly on paper, the method of planning is essentially the same. Planning looks ahead and makes the best use of manpower, money, material and equipment.

Let's say you've planned to take a business administration certificate program in the evenings at your local university. Taking two subjects per semester in the evening, you're looking at several years of hard work. So, this would be a long-term planning problem. Because it's a long-term project, you might feel discouraged about starting such a complex task or reluctant to make a commitment of this size.

If you break it down into small segments (one session at a time) you'll only have to deal with a portion of the overall project at one time. In the meantime, forget about the other subjects until it's time to take them. This way, you'll be able to give undivided attention to the one you're dealing with right now. You can then tackle portions of it, and it won't appear as overwhelming as you thought.

Would this be a tangible or intangible problem?

It's an intangible problem because it does not involve a physical object, but instead deals with behaviour, knowledge and feelings.

The Importance of Planning:

If proper planning is taken, the need for problem-solving may not occur in the first place.

Can you think of instances in your own work area where there was a lack of planning? What were some of the problems it caused? Here are examples of some that can happen due to lack of planning:

Failure to get reports out on time.

Time is wasted.

Overtime necessary *"to catch up."*

Results in bottlenecks to others.

Staff left with nothing to do while waiting for assignments.

Disorganised employees; and

Lose clients.

Planning what should be done each day, each week, each month can be tackled as follows:

Write down your routine duties

Write down your periodic duties

It's important at this point that you have an accurate, up-to-date job description so you and your supervisor are clear about what your responsibilities are.

Many companies do not have proper job descriptions. They expect a simple paragraph to describe what their employees do to complete their tasks. Then they have the audacity to conduct performance appraisals when neither the supervisors nor the employee, have nothing in writing about what they are evaluating. Many performance appraisals evaluate subjective, rather than objective issues. No wonder there's chaos in some companies!

Job Descriptions

Every position (not just groups of positions) should have accurate, up-too-date job descriptions. Many companies update their job descriptions when they conduct their annual performance appraisals. These companies fully understand that if the employee doesn't know what they're supposed to do (and their supervisor doesn't know either) - how can supervisors possibly evaluate how well their employees are performing their tasks?

Job descriptions should include all the information you'd want, should you be filling the position. <u>Remember, that Job Descriptions describe the position - not the person filling it.</u>

All Job Descriptions must have:

1. General paragraph describing the position.

2. KPIs (Key Performance Indicators). These are the main functions of the job – what tasks must be accomplished by this position.

3. List of tasks to meet the KPIs.

4. Standards of performance for each task.

Standards of performance:

Job descriptions and performance appraisals should both have detailed standards of performance to clarify what is expected of employees. A Standard of Performance is a yardstick against which performance in a part of a job is measured. It's usually a series of brief statements of the quality and quantity expected within specific time frames and identifies the costs (in time and/or money).

For example:

Task:

Hire three sales personnel

Standard of performance:

Hire three sales personnel who have a minimum of three years' directly related experience by May 1, 20___, at a basic salary range of $40,000 to $50,000 per annum.

Quality:

3 years' directly related experience. (You'd have to establish what *"directly related experience"* really means).

Quantity:

3 sales personnel

Time:

By May 1, 20 ___.

Cost:

Salary range of $40,000 to $50,000 per annum.

When setting Standards of Performance

Use the performance of other people in similar situations. (Watch you don't choose a high or low achiever's performance as *"average!"*).

Engineered or prevailing standards.

Employees' past performance on the job as shown from their previous performance appraisals.

What managers and employees negotiate as reasonable.

Advantages of setting standards of performance:

A worker who knows his or her job has certain specific standards, is always aware of how s/he is doing. Employees can rate their own job effectiveness and start improvement in unsatisfactory areas without waiting for appraisals from their managers.

Standards of Performance enable the manager to evaluate his or her whole department realistically. Managers can spot areas where individual employees need improvement, take steps to improve the whole group, and recognise superior performance.

Standards make it possible to base performance rating on something more objective than personality traits and surface impressions (i.e. judgement, initiative, interpersonal skills, attitude). They keep the personalities out of it and deal only with the actual output of the employee.

Sample headings on Job Descriptions are:

Title of Position:

Position #:

Location:

Hours of work:

Department, branch or unit:

Reports to:

Job Summary: (in paragraph form - just giving brief description of the position).

Duties and Responsibilities: (showing percentage of time spent on each duty or weighting in importance.)

Start with Key Performance Indicators (KPIs). These are the major functions of the job. For instance:

Responsible for all company training.

Under each KPI, list all the tasks that must be performed to achieve the KPI.

For instance:

Ensure that all supervisors and managers receive our approved 3-day supervisory training course by June 1st, 20____ for a yearly cost of less than $120,000.

Under each task, list the standards of performance relating to that task.

For example:

Quality: Approved 3-day supervisory training course.

Quantity: All supervisors and managers.

Time: June 1st, 20____.

Cost: Less than $120,000.

Work Complexity: (such as choice of action, consequences of error, difficulty or work pressures, contacts, confidentiality).

Supervision received: (level, how much independent action).

Whom position supervises: (Titles of positions direct or indirect supervision. Do they assign work? Review work? Conduct performance appraisals? Discipline subordinates?)

Working conditions: (be specific about adverse conditions).

Equipment used: (be specific).

Qualifications required: such as formal education, experience, specific skills, licenses or certificates, physical requirements (i.e. employee must be able to handle packages weighing up to 10 kg).

Probationary period:

Promotional opportunities:

No more than 10% of their duties should be identified as: "Other Duties as Assigned."

If the employee performs the duty every day, every week, or once every year - it should be on his or her position description.

Why is probationary period included on a position description? While an employee is on probation, there's far less paperwork should you wish to fire them because of inadequate performance. The employee would probably want to know how long the probationary period is, because many companies don't put employees on full company benefits until their probationary period is over.

How long should a probationary period be? Most companies have anywhere from three months to one year. If employees must wait a full year to receive company benefits (which can be 30 to 50 per cent of their base salary) they'd miss a lot of extra money. It's also a long time to be on *"tender hooks,"* wondering if they're going to be accepted as a full-time employee. Some union agreements stipulate set probationary periods.

Promotional opportunities need to be listed as well. If candidates are *"fast-trackers,"* you'll lose them if they're placed in a dead-ended position with little chance of promotion. On the other hand, many people are not *"fast trackers"* and would be content staying in one position for a long time.

Sample Job Description

[Company Logo]

Position Title

Salary Range

Department/Location

Number of Reports: Direct? Indirect?

Reports to: (title)

Working Conditions:

[Work setting, stresses of the job, deadline-prone activities, requirement to deal with difficult clients, colleagues, pressures from many departments, quotas to meet, inside, outside, special conditions etc.]

Work Complexity:

[Such as choice of action, consequences of error, work pressures, contacts, confidentiality]

Position Summary:

[In paragraph form – just giving a brief description of the position]

List Key Performance Indicators/Objectives:

1. Identify the Key Performance Indicator. [i.e.: Hire competent staff].

2. List the tasks that will be performed to reach the Key Performance Indicator.

3. Give a weight to the importance of each task. (Total for ALL tasks performed on Job Description must not be more than 100%.)

4. Make sure each task has Standards of Performance i.e.:

5. When setting standards of performance, keep in mind how you will measure whether the task has been completed properly

Key Performance Indicator/Objective

(Hire 3 sales representatives)

Weight of each task: [how important is this responsibility compared to other responsibilities?]

Tasks:

Standards of Performance

Key Performance Indicator/Objective

(Hire 2 Classification Clerk 1 staff)

Weight of each task: [how important is this responsibility compared to other responsibilities]

Tasks:

Standards of Performance

[Add other tasks to list and go to the next items]

Decision-making authority:

Key Customers: Internal? External?

Equipment Used:

Probationary Period:

Promotional Opportunities: [What is the career path for this position?]

Medical Requirements of Position: [Be careful with this one – it must be a true requirement].

Key Competencies:

> Experience/Qualifications:
> Knowledge:
> Skills:
> Attributes/Behaviours].

Testing abilities of employees:

To determine individual needs when hiring and for determining future training needs, a company may administer the following more objective tests:

General intellectual abilities: These are not typical I.Q. tests, but are more job-related and determine verbal comprehension and reasoning abilities.

Aptitude tests: Determine a person's capacity to obtain new levels of knowledge, skills and attitudes from training.

Achievement tests: Measures what an employee knows, understands or can do in relation to specific areas of knowledge or skill.

Motor skill tests: Involve physical agility, manual dexterity and sense of hearing, vision and touch. These are used where motor abilities are essential for successful completion of duties of a position.

Interests and motivation tests: Are difficult tests to assess because people tend to give answers, they think are expected of them. To obtain correct assessment, questions must be skilfully worded. The person evaluating these tests requires considerable training themselves.

Interpersonal and leadership skills: Assessed from work history and references from present and former supervisors.

Personal history data: Begins with the application form or resume and information from an employee's personnel file. This information includes previous education, experience, credentials, membership and occasionally reference checks.

Current performance and potential: Assessed by performance appraisals and employee's capability for learning.

Dimensions tested:

These are more subjective and only used in conjunction with objective information gathered. They are valuable for determining training needs in areas that are not as tangible to evaluate as objective ones:

Speaking ability: Ability to effectively express oneself in both individual and group situations.

Listening ability: Ability to pick out important information in oral communication.

Writing ability: Ability to express ideas in a clear, concise, grammatically correct manner.

Reading ability: Ability to obtain facts and comprehend meaning in written communication.

Ability to analyse: Ability to identify and interpret the key elements of a situation, concept or problem.

Judgement: Ability to evaluate situations and/or information and reach logical conclusions.

Decisiveness: Readiness to make decisions on the basis of sound judgment.

Plan and organise: Ability to effectively plan and organise their own work and direct or assist others in planning and organising their work.

Delegate: Ability to delegate tasks in a manner conducive to effectiveness and subordinate development.

Control: Ability to effectively use administrative controls for evaluation, auditing and monitoring functions.

Leadership: Ability to guide a group or individual to where they can effectively accomplish a task.

Flexibility: Ability to modify their approach and/or behaviour as required.

Empathy: Awareness, understanding and consideration of the needs and feelings of others.

Initiative: Ability to motivate themselves to take positive action and have a *"sense of urgency."*

Tolerance to stress: Ability to maintain expected performance levels under stress.

Co-operative philosophy: Ability to perceive and show positive reaction to current needs and future expectations of the company.

Creativeness: Ability to generate imaginative solutions to problem situations.

Planning Factors:

If you are a supervisor facing the task of updating your job descriptions, you might find the following information will help you tackle this task.

Factor 1: What needs to be done?

Determine if the tasks planned for the day are, Routine, Periodic or Special. i.e.:

Routine: Those things that the staff member does every day that might consist of keeping on top of regular work (uses 60 to 70 percent of his/her time).

Examples:

Getting the day's work started.

Checking work left over from yesterday.

Giving information.

Checking incoming mail and e-mail.

Periodic: Those duties or tasks that occur at regular intervals such as weekly, monthly, specific workday of the month etc. (Uses 20 to 25 percent of his/her time).

Examples:

Weekly or monthly reports.

Inventory checks.

Staff meetings.

Safety meetings.

Updating job descriptions and

Conducting Performance appraisals.

Special: Those could be things that could be done to improve their work (can be above and beyond the call of duty). These could be ideas suggestions and proposed new ways of doing a task or special project.

Examples:

Defining better ways of completing a task.

Completing special projects.

Setting up new policies and procedures.

Revising or reducing reports or forms.

Write down all the routine, periodic and special duties that they do. Now do the same for yourself. If your company doesn't have job descriptions, you're well on your way to producing them!

Factor 2: How is task to be completed?

What's your unit producing or servicing?

What staff function is being offered?

How do you measure your staff's performance?

How does your manager measure your performance?

Factor 3: Who's to do it?

A job skills inventory sheet is often a good tool to answer this question. A job inventory can assist by:

Showing turnover due to transfers, separations and retirements.

Identifying vulnerable areas where there's a minimum coverage of responsibility.

Establishing a training pattern for new workers; and

Identifying the need for job rotation so you adequately cover all positions (especially those affected because of staff illness).

Factor 4 - When should it be done?

When is the best time to do it?

Should you combine the task with other tasks?

Should it be done before or after some other tasks?

Factor 5 - Where's it to be done?

Where's the task being done?

Where else could it be done?

Where's the best place to do it?

Factor 6 - What results are achieved?

Cross-training eliminates vacancies due to illness.

Bottlenecks are eliminated.

Fewer surprises.

Fewer crises and

Better utilisation of staff, materials and money.

Job Skills Inventory Chart:

Factor 3 mentioned a Jobs Skills Inventory Chart. Here's a sample job skills inventory chart for a Mail Room Unit.

Worker: Bill Adams

>Responsibilities: Machine maintenance

Worker: Pat Elum

>Responsibilities: Mail sorting, Word Processing

Worker: Stan Ward

>Responsibilities: Postage Machine

Worker: Lyle Harris

>Responsibilities: Mail delivery

Worker: Mary Mooney

>Responsibilities: Mail sorting, Postal Zones

Worker: Helen Pepper

>Responsibilities: Word processing

Worker: Frank Ricker

>Responsibilities: Mail sorting, Machine maintenance

Worker: Chuck Sweeney

>Responsibilities: Mail Sorting, Postage Machine, Postal Zones, Machine Maintenance

Worker: Clara Anders

>Responsibilities: Word Processing

As you examine this job skills inventory chart, what are some strengths and weaknesses of this group should concern the supervisor?

Strengths:

Lots of word processors (too many?)

3 machine maintenance people.

Relief help for mail sorting, postage machine and postal zoning.

Weaknesses:

Too many responsibilities for Chuck?

No relief for mail delivery and addressograph operator.

Boredom for Stan, Helen, Clara and Lyle.

Complete a Job Skills Inventory Chart for your area. What discrepancies does it point out? Should you be contemplating job rotation or cross-training? What if one of your staff was sick, could you place another experienced worker in his/her place?

The value of Job Rotation

Job rotation often reduces the boredom of repetitive kinds of tasks. There's another spin-off benefit - that of having more than one person qualified to take over the duties of a position. Should an employee be on vacation or ill, another can take over his/her duties reducing any backlog. When supervisors know the talents and abilities of their staff, they can delegate work to those who appear to like that kind of task. Giving employees new tasks that keep them learning, will also remove the tedium of their work.

Supervisors should resist hiring either over- or underqualified staff. Over-qualified staff will likely be bored with their job within months. If you've made this faux pas, the employee will probably want a promotion in a hurry. You may lose them to another company unless you allow them that opportunity. Under-qualified staff will be playing the game of *"catch-up"* which could be very stressful for them. You'll have to give them extra training and time to catch up with the position expectations. Consider extending their probationary period longer than normal, so you have more opportunity to see if they can handle the position before making them permanent employees.

Manpower planning:

When determining training needs it's important to evaluate the present situation. Companies use manpower planning to compare the demands of the corporation vs. the supply of manpower available. This defines immediate needs and establishes long-range requirements.

Demand: Refers to the perceived demands of an organisation determined by budgetary requests, predicted expansions and changes in technology (usually determined in five-year forecasts).

Supply: The existing supply of manpower less turnover, retirement, attrition, etc. Often companies have senior people who are ready to retire. They suddenly realise there's no one to replace them or they realise there'll be a gap if they promote someone to a higher level. Manpower planning keeps this from happening and uses and expands the skills of existing employees.

Keeping alive employee's desire to contribute

Possibly the problem you face is a lethargic de-motivated employee. How can you solve this problem and help the employee?

1. Provide an atmosphere of approval:

An atmosphere of approval can be created by the following steps:

a) Recognise the importance of employee suggestions.

b) Listen to them - if not now, arrange for it later.

c) Avoid Progress Killers.

d) Explain why new ideas won't work.

e) If employee gives a good idea, implement it as soon as possible and give employee credit for the idea.

2. Give employee meaningful participation:

The evidence is pretty convincing, that whenever people can influence their own work in a way that provides them with an opportunity to have a decisive voice, they will be more interested and involved. Employees will feel their participation is meaningful if you practice the following:

a) Analyse your job and decide which tasks can be moved downward.

b) Be willing to take the risk of more job involvement by your subordinates.

c) Encourage your employees to volunteer for assignments they can handle.

d) Don't con your employees with the feeling that they're giving meaningful participation when a decision has already been made.

e) When your decision has been influenced by the employee's ideas - tell him/her.

3. Give performance feedback:

Some supervisors (and thank goodness they're getting fewer and fewer), believe that the yearly performance appraisal is all that's necessary, otherwise the employees are *"on their own."* Employees that work for this kind of supervisor find:

a) They don't have a job description.

b) They aren't sure what's expected of them, therefore have no objectives to meet.

c) The seldom hear about what they did right (except silence), but appear to hear lots about what they did wrong.

4. Give consistent discipline:

If supervisors show favouritism or have a personality clash with employees, consistent discipline usually is a mirage. To ensure consistent discipline, a supervisor must:

a) Review rules and standards regularly to evaluate their relevancy.

b) Ensure rules are known and understood by all employees.

c) Reward or punish consistently.

d) Be aware of extenuating circumstances.

e) Document your action and reasoning you used to make decisions.

f) Follow-up to see if situation has improved.

5. *Give them the right of appeal:*

This is used only after serious attempts have been made by both the supervisor and the employee to settle a dispute. A third person or mediator, to call upon, is usually a personnel manager or union rep who can remain objective about the conflict. Companies that don't offer this right of appeal are missing a very effective management tool. Supervisors/managers are advised as follows:

a) You're not always right, this procedure protects you and your employees.

b) Be sure to listen carefully.

c) Welcome this appeal process - you may need to use it yourself some day.

Have you ever lost a good employee because there was no *"Right of Appeal"* in your company?

Many companies recognise that there are problems like this where employees and supervisors alike need an impartial person to intervene to help them settle the dispute. This can be a Human Resources manager or any other trained negotiator who can remain objective about the conflict. Companies that don't offer the *"right of appeal"* are missing a very effective management tool.

Problems with Time Wasters

Possibly your problem is dealing with staff who waste their and others time resulting in extra budget costs because of that wasted time. Here are some suggestions on solving that kind of problem:

1. Telephone Interruptions:

a) Distinguish between business and personal calls.

b) Keep business calls to business matters.

c) Set a time limit to conversations.

d) When making phone calls - have a list of information that must be discussed.

2. Drop-in visitors:

a) Distinguish between businesss and personal visitors.

b) Have receptionist screen visitors before they see you.

c) Discourage socializing - continue with your work.

d) Be honest with visitors. state for instance, *"I only have a few minutes - how can I help you."* - and stick to it!

3. Ineffective delegation:

a) Talk with your supervisor to see if you can have someone else handle a duty that you feel doesn't fit your position.

b) Delegate duties to subordinates that can do them best.

4. Meetings:

a) Be sure your attendance serves a purpose.

b) Don't call unnecessary meetings.

c) If your schedule is too busy - send a representative to get the information you'll need.

5. Lack of objectives/priorities and planning:

a) Keep up-to-date job descriptions.

b) Define priority items.

c) Make sure objectives are known and handled by subordinates.

d) Use effective planning strategies.

6. Dealing with crisis situations:

a) Assess how often it happens.

b) Find a system for dealing with crisis.

c) Make sure objectives are known and handled by subordinates.

d) Use effective planning strategies.

7. *Attempting too much at once:*

a) Set objectives and priorities.

b) Make daily *"To Do"* lists.

c) Delegate properly.

8. *Cluttered desk – personal disorganisation:*

a) Allow time to organise - it will save time later.

b) Minimise paperwork.

c) Use verbal communication as often as possible.

d) Put away anything that you're not working on at present.

e) Everything has a place.

9. *Indecision/procrastination:*

a) Take an assertiveness course.

b) Daily *"To Do"* lists keep you on track.

c) Ask others to help you determine when you're indecisive or are procrastinating.

d) Have faith that you have the ability to do the job.

10. *Inability to say "No":*

a) Take an assertiveness course.

b) You can't please all of the people all the time.

c) Recognise traps.

d) Offer alternative solutions.

e) Assess consequences of saying *"Yes."*

f) Every *"No"* does NOT have to be explained to others.

g) Count to ten before saying *"Yes."*

h) Better to do less well, than more poorly.

11. *Unclear communication/instructio:*

a) Develop listening skills

b) Practice paraphrasing and feedback.

c) Repeat instructions.

12. *Confused responsibility and authority:*

a) Have up-to-date job descriptions for yourself and your subordinates.

b) Determine your subordinate's level of responsibility and authority.

13. *Delayed, inaccurate information:*

a) Check information source - don't listen to the grapevine.

b) Check for bottleneck employees.

c) Practice listening skills.

d) Use paraphrasing and feedback.

e) Speak, don't write except to back-up information.

14. *Lack of self-discipline:*

a) Keep a daily *"To Do"* list.

b) Set objectives and plan daily.

c) Set priorities.

d) Schedule unpleasant tasks **First**.

15. *Leaving tasks unfinished:*

a) Same as #14.

16. *Untrained, inadequate staff:*

a) Utilise *"old timers"* in your department for information.

b) Be aware of training needs of your subordinates.

c) Have them ready for promotional opportunities.

d) Have open-door policy for employees who seek your help.

17. *Socializing:*

a) Control the urge.

b) Monitor your staff for socializing.

c) Keep your own socializing to coffee breaks and lunch.

d) Keep busy!

Solve this problem:

Six months ago, Phil Evers was promoted to the position of foreman - Plant Maintenance at the Nyack Spinning Mill. He had been a mechanic on the company's maintenance force for almost 20 years.

Phil was a good worker and everyone knew it. He enjoyed his work and thoroughly understood the operation, maintenance and repair of the many pieces of mechanical equipment in use throughout the plant. Because of his technical competence, he had the respect of the rest of the crew. It was the main reason he had been picked to be foreman.

Not having supervised people before, Phil was told by his Operations Manager, John Lumley, that he would now be expected to do much less of the actual work himself, and instead, train and direct the work of the people under him.

At first, Phil tried to act the way he thought a supervisor should. For example, he started wearing a tie every day to work so he could look the part. He also tried to organise his day so he could spend most of his time doing paperwork. It wasn't long, however, before complaints started to come in from the production floor. Machinery was breaking down and production was held up because repairs weren't being made fast enough.

When Phil sent his men to make repairs, they often called back to him for help because they didn't know how to fix the equipment themselves. Sometimes Phil could help matters by giving directions over the phone, but more often he went down and did the job himself.

Gradually, Phil spent more and more time away from his desk, and soon he was back in his work clothes. It seemed as if things went better when he was there himself to keep the equipment running, although he was hard-pressed to keep up with the growing work load.

Phil's crew started grumbling that he was too possessive with the machinery. They claimed he was deliberately not showing them how to do the work because he liked to do it himself.

John Lumley talked to Phil several times about the situation. After each talk, Phil spent more of his time *"supervising"* and less time *"doing,"* but then slowly slipped back into his old habit of doing most of the tough jobs himself.

In the face of the continuing complaints from production, John Lumley knew he had to act, but didn't know what to do. He realised that Phil was an excellent mechanic, but also realised he wasn't adequately performing his supervisory duties.

Question #1: What was the main problem?

Participants at my sessions normally chose the following as the main problem:

Were there more than one?

1. Phil Evers had not been trained to handle his new position by former supervisor or John Lumley
2. Phil didn't know how to supervise his staff
3. Phil didn't know how to train his staff

Question #2: If you were John Lumley, what would you do about Phil Evers?

1. Send Phil to a supervisory training program.
2. Send Phil to a supervisory training program.
3. Help Phil put together a training program for his staff and assist him in the training

However, looking at this problem from the company's point of view - it would be much more important to them to raise production levels. Everyone would have to pitch in (including John Lumley) to accomplish that. Then they could tackle the other problems.

So, pretending that you owned the company would have given you the correct answer. Try to remember this when solving company problems.

CHAPTER THREE

RESISTANCE TO YOUR PLANS

Many workers object to job rotation, but what they're likely objecting to is their fear of change. To overcome this fear of change:

The Change Process:

People go through four basic stages when they have changes made in anything they do. Supervisors and trainers must be aware of this, because they will *"slip back"* to doing it the old way if not stopped.

Unfreezing: Happens when you *"unfreeze"* their regular way of doing things that allows the acceptance of new ideas. This involves breaking down of old ways of doing things and can involve customs and traditions.

Changing: This provides a new pattern of behaviour, identifies a new way of doing something. Before approaching anyone with a change, identify the driving forces and find ways to overcome the restraining forces. Describing the advantages of the new system is essential for success.

Refreezing: The new idea replaces the old one and the new way is *"frozen,"* so employees don't revert to the old way. Die-hards will resist and try to do it the *"old way"* so you must be wary of these people.

Commitment: People are ready to make plans that utilise the new way, to set and implement long-range plans.

When implementing a change, you feel may meet with resistance (and even those you don't) do advance planning. Make a list of:

> Driving forces in favour of the plan succeeding and benefits that will result (brainstorm).

Restraining forces against the plan succeeding and things standing in the way (brainstorm).

Find solutions to restraining forces.

Put solution on paper for easy reference.

Introduce the change.

Evaluate the effectiveness of your planning and the change itself.

New systems, methods and designs won't work unless you get people to accept new ideas, so you may have to sell your ideas. This is where planning comes in.

For Example: You've found a faster way to process client's orders. Before explaining the new system to others, prepare by:

Writing down the existing way. (Its advantages and disadvantages).

Writing down the new way (Its advantages and disadvantages).

Anticipate that George will object by saying *"But we've always done it this way. Twenty people will have to learn a new way of doing it."*

Your answer could be (giving concrete facts) *"Here's how much time we'll save by doing it the new way. I've determined that we'll save 5 minutes per order. As there are about 1,000 orders processed per month that's a saving of 5,000 minutes or 250 minutes per employee per month. This means that every employee will have an extra 4 hours and 10 minutes to work on other tasks per month. This amounts to a saving of $_____."*

If there are further objections from George say: *"George, why do you feel we should continue doing it the old say?"* George is not likely to have facts ready as you've had. Remember however, that if the new procedure doesn't work - you won't look good - so do considerable planning before implementing this kind of change.

Progress killers

"It isn't in the budget."

"We tried that before."

"It doesn't fit our program."

"Has anyone else tried it?"

"It's against or policy."

"It costs too much."

"The union will scream."

"Upper management will scream."

"Management will never buy it."

"We don't have the authority."

"Not that again!"

"Let's give it more thought."

"We did all right without it."

And the big one:

"We've always done it this way!"

Team Changes

It's often necessary in business for groups or teams of people to make difficult decisions and implement change. This can bring out a lot of problems with the participants who have differing points of view on how things should be done.

1. What kinds of problems have you run into when working in a team atmosphere?

2. Did the team leader do a good job of focusing the group on making decisions towards change?

The leader's role in any group situation, is to help achieve the objectives. Other functions include:

Planning for Team Changes

This usually starts with meeting agendas that may or may not have input from team members. This agenda arranges where and when the meeting will be held, who will speak, what is discussed and how long each topic is given for discussion.

During the meeting the team leader must plan how to deal with such situations as:

1. Is the group moving towards meeting the objectives?

2. Are individual needs being met, as well as group needs?

3. Is the meeting climate psychologically safe for change?

4. Are they working harmoniously with each other?

5. Are the group's unique talents and abilities being utilised?

If members of the team are subordinates of yours, make sure you check their personnel file to see where their areas of expertise lie. One may be an exceptional organiser, so naturally you would delegate things that would bring out this talent. However, if you were not aware of this skill, you may delegate the responsibility to a less qualified member.

If you don't have access to personnel files (possibly person works for another department or company), ask person to volunteer for things s/he thinks s/he can handle. Try to provide an atmosphere that:

a) Shows people they are important. Don't interrupt - listen to what they have to say. Occasionally you will have to reject ideas, but never reject people. When rejecting ideas, explain why. Never label people in any way - i.e. *"John, that was a stupid thing to suggest!"* Make sure members know you're rejecting their ideas - not them. You do this by encouraging further input and ideas from them.

b) Encourage an atmosphere conducive to change. Show them you encourage new ideas and ways of doing things. Bring out their creativity, especially when dealing with problems. That's when most innovative ideas surface.

c) Implement *"brainstorming"* sessions when solving problems. Encourage a free-wheeling atmosphere where no one is threatened by any idea they may initiate. This process enables you to have *"Plan B"* on the back burner if *"Plan A"* doesn't work.

d) If they stray off topic, bring them back with such statements as *"We're getting off track here. We were discussing... Does anyone have an idea?"*

6. Overcome cultural or personality differences.

If a personality clash happens at a meeting, stop the members involved. Suggest that you have a further meeting with the people involved to discuss the problems identified by the clash. Then bring them back on track by suggesting, *"Let's get back to the topic we were discussing. I need all of you to concentrate on reaching the objectives of this meeting."*

If the leader is dealing with people of different cultural backgrounds, it's important that s/he understands what makes that person tick. Read a very good book called *"The Silent Language"* by Dr. Edward T. Hall. Blatant discrimination of meeting members should be immediately discouraged. Jokes at the expense of someone else are not jokes at all. Discourage such comments by stating, *"I don't think that was funny, Paul."* If Paul states, *"I was only kidding."* reply by stating, *"Paul, if your comments are harmless, then they're pointless, so keep your thoughts to yourself."*

7. Evaluate.

The leader must constantly assess the feelings of the group, as well as the group's progress towards accomplishing the task. S/he may have to table some issues for a later meeting, because crucial information was not available.

8. Follow-up.

Meeting objections head-on:

The following checklist will help you cope with objections more effectively.

1. Pinpoint the objection - spell it out in clear and concise language.

2. Don't take the voiced objections of others for granted. People sometimes voice one complaint to mask another they'd prefer to conceal.

3. Work out a practical way of erasing the objection if possible.

4. If you're unable to remove it, try to find a way to counteract it.

5. Anticipate and prepare for as many possible objections as you can. Develop a plan for handling each. (Rehearse).

6. Rally enough benefits to win the person's support and co-operation despite the objection.

7. Try to find a way to get around the objection or to minimise its adverse effect.

8. Collect as much irrefutable evidence as you can; to convince the person you're trying to sell that his/her objection is unreasonable (if such is the case).

9. Find a way to ease the person's mind, by making it less risky to go along with you despite their objection.

10. Spoon-feed your idea or proposal on a gradual basis.

11. Don't try to get immediate acceptance or compliance. The objection may be nothing more than a delaying tactic, the person's natural resistance to change.

12. Consider bringing up significant objections yourself instead of waiting for the other person to do it.

Making changes happen

It can be a difficult process if you have a new idea and want others to use it. Objections may be received from peer groups, other supervisors or your own staff.

Here's a guide that you can use when making changes (it's like the problem-solving guide) to help you deal with change. Write down:

Step 1: The existing way

We have 40 parking stalls available for staff parking.

Step 2: The proposed new way

We must reduce this number to 30 parking stalls.

Step 3: Identify how it is done now.

What's happening?

We have 40 parking stalls available for staff parking.

Where is it happening?

In the staff parking area.

When it occurs?

Daily parking provided for 3 shifts (120 staff)

Who's involved?

Senior staff.

How does it happen?

Seniority list determines those who can have stalls.

Step 4: Identify the proposed new way:

What's happening?

We have only 30 parking stalls available for staff parking (reduction of 10 stalls).

Where is it happening?

In the staff parking area.

When it occurs?

Daily parking provided for 3 shifts (90 staff). (30 staff will have to find parking elsewhere).

Who's involved?

Senior staff.

How does it happen?

Seniority list determines those who can have stalls.

Step 5: List the Driving Forces (Benefits when the change is made)

No confusion as to who will or will not have a parking stall.

We'll be able to use the extra space for visitors (clients).

Less hostility from clients and customers because visitor parking will now be available.

Step 6: List the Restraining Forces (Obstacles to making the change)

a) 30 staff who have parking stalls will have to find parking elsewhere.

b) Problems with union.

c) Sour grapes and possible sabotage on the part of employees.

d) Resentment towards those who still have parking stalls.

e) Guilt feelings on the part of those who still have parking stalls.

Step 7: List all the possible solutions to solve the restraining forces (Brainstorm)

a) Make a list of alternative parking in the area.

b) Have a meeting with the union representatives - ask for their co-operation during implementation of the change.

c) Call a meeting with affected employees to explain the reasons for the change (better customer relations - increased sales and profits). Explain that you will pay for their parking at an alternative nearby site.

d) Provide an extra perk to those losing parking stalls - possibly give each person who must go to an alternative site a fire extinguisher or first-aid kit for their vehicle.

e) There shouldn't be any guilt feelings if the above is put into place.

Step 8: Formulate an Action Plan:

Step or Action: Determine which employees will have to give up parking stalls
Date or Time Limit: Today
People to Involve: Me
Resources Required: Seniority list

Step or Action: Find and choose alternative parking
Date or Time Limit: Tomorrow
People to Involve: Personal Assistant
Resources Required: Time

Step or Action: Meet with union representatives
Date or Time Limit: Tomorrow
People to Involve: Union Reps – me
Resources Required: Time, preparation

Step or Action: Obtain samples of fire extinguishers and first aid kits
Date or Time Limit: Friday, the 6th
People to Involve: Personal
Resources Required: Time, cost of samples

Step or Action: Call meeting with affected employees
Date or Time Limit: Monday the 9th
People to Involve: Employees, me
Resources Required: Preparation, list of options

Step 9: Implement your action plan

Meeting with employees held (date).

Step 10: Evaluate the success of your action plan

Employees were upset initially, but when they learned that we would pay for nearby parking for them and provide either a fire extinguisher or first aid kit for their vehicles they agreed to accept the change.

Conflict Resolution:

Possibly your problem-solving involves a conflict with one or more other people. Whenever conflict occurs, it's helpful to consider the four basic approaches to resolving conflicts:

Competition Approach: These are:

"Win-Lose" situations - One person or group wins, the other loses.

"Might makes right" - This could be the status of a person in a company.

"Winner takes all" - Another win-lose situation.

"Survival of the Fittest" - One-upmanship.

Accommodation Approach: These are:

"Yield-lose" situations - Passive behaviour. Person doesn't actively participate.

"Kill your enemies with kindness." - This too is passive – a form of passive resistance.

Compromising Approach: These are:

"Sharing, negotiating, bargaining."

"Win some - lose some."

"Splitting the difference."

"You rub my back - I'll rub yours."

"Democracy."

Collaboration Approach: These are:

"Let's work together" – teamwork.

"Two heads are better than one."

The last one - Collaboration Approach is the best conflict resolution approach. There are no competitive feelings in this approach, rather a feeling of co-operation between members of the team - camaraderie. All members are open to negotiate. This attitude uses all the talents of the group without losing the individualities of the members. There are no negatives - only positives. It's a win-win approach.

Teamwork: *Is a group of people working honestly and affably with one another.*

The Effective Group

Here are the criteria that make for an effective group:

1. Have a clear understanding of their purposes and goals.

2. Are flexible in selecting their procedures as they work towards their goals.

3. Have achieved a high degree of communication and understanding among the members.

4. Communication of personal feelings and attitudes, as well as ideas, occurs in a direct and open fashion because they are considered important to the work of the group.

5. Can initiate and fulfill effective decision-making, carefully considering minority viewpoints and securing the commitment of all members to important decisions.

6. Achieve an appropriate balance between group productivity and the satisfaction of individual needs.

7. Provide the sharing of leadership responsibilities of group members so that all members are concerned about the contribution of ideas, elaborating and clarifying the ideas of others, giving opinions, testing the feasibility of potential decisions, and in other ways helping others in the group work towards completion of tasks.

8. Have a high degree of cohesiveness, but not to the point of stifling individual freedom, and submerging individual differences.

9. Make intelligent use of the different abilities of its members.

10. Are not dominated by the leader or by any of the members.

11. Can be objective about reviewing its own processes. Can face their problems and adjust to needed modifications in their operations.

12. Maintain a balance between emotional and rational behaviour, channelling emotions towards productive group effort.

Normal Problem-Solving Steps:

1. Problem definition

2. Idea production

These are two steps used by creative people who use their right side of their brains.

3. Idea Evaluation

4. Decision

5. Detail and Optimizing

6.Action planning

7. Implementation and feedback

These are used by people in control situations who are using the left side of their brains.

The Chicken Problem

Let's see how well you can use the creative side of your brain.

For example:

Suppose you live on the outskirts of the city with a nice lawn and garden (of which you are very proud). Your neighbours keep chickens (legally) which, because of the absence of a fence, come into your yard, make a mess and eat the seeds you've planted. They also scratch and dig up your lawn.

You have spoken to your neighbours about it, but although they're very sympathetic and apologetic, they have done nothing. You can't afford to build a fence yourself. What should you do? Discussion of the problem with your family and friends through brainstorming, has produced the following suggestions:

a) Dig a ditch and fill it with water

b) Buy a dog

c) Catch the chickens and cook them

d) Sell the house and move

e) Ask the neighbours to share in the cost of building a fence

f) Shoot the chickens

g) Take the neighbours to court

h) Let a fox loose at night time

i) Replace the lawn and garden with crazy-paving or concrete

j) Spread poisoned corn over your garden

k) Plant a hedge

l) Buy a *"bird-scarer"* (a device that goes *"bang"* at irregular intervals)

Now decide how the following fits with the course of action you chose:

* Relevance

* Practicability

* Desirability

* Cost

* Legality

* Time

* Social acceptability

What option did you choose? Here are the types:

a) Accommodating

b) Competition

c) Competition

d) Accommodating

e) Collaboration

f) Competition

g) Competition

h) Competition

i) Accommodating

j) Competition

k) Collaboration

l) Accommodation

The best suggestion would be k) Plant a hedge.

How did you do? Did you choose a competitive or accommodating choice?

Conflict can be a good thing. It provides:

An opportunity to try new ideas

Challenges members to do something better

It expands the horizons of those involved

Think of problems your company has faced in the past. Has this led to new and innovative ways of dealing with situations?

One asset for creative thinking is to have a good sense of visualisation.

Visualisation

We use visualization when we look in a drawer for a potato peeler, or into a closet for a certain outfit. We see in our mind's eye what it looks like, the shape, the colour and the size. But how does visualization differ from fantasizing? How do these two differ?

Those who fantasise usually aren't in touch with reality. These are the people who really expect to win a lottery when their chances of doing so are so slim that they would be better to bank the money spent on tickets and allow it to earn interest or invest it. Those who fantasise often try to reach unreachable goals and make a stab at reaching those goals but stop as soon as they run into resistance. These are often negative thinkers (or become so, because they didn't obtain their fantasies.)

The positive thinker who uses visualization, sees themselves reaching their goal or solving their problem, but also clearly identify obstructions they may face along the way. Instead of quitting when they hit those barricades, they identify how they can go under, over, around or through the obstacle. Then they identify the next obstacle, overcome it, and keep on until they reach their goal or solve their problem. This is done **before** their project or goal is underway. If too many obstacles appear, the project can be dropped without wasting real effort. However, they must watch that they don't *"cop out"* and give up to soon.

When trying to change things or solve a problem I always ask myself two questions:

What have I got to gain?

What have I got to lose?

If I have lots to gain and little to lose – I usually go for it.

Positive Thinking - I will succeed because...

Negative Thinking - I will fail because...

If only... I should have...

Many people spend their lives reliving the past. They get into a mental rut that concentrates on what was, rather than what will be. Many of their comments start out with the prefaces, *'I should have...'* or *'If only I could...'*

Here's a story of a woman who has used those two prefaces for most of her life:

Celia married and stayed at home with her four children. She suffered from severe depression but did not receive professional help for it. Suddenly, at the age of 43 her husband Roger told her that he wanted a divorce because he wanted to marry someone else. Celia had not been aware there was trouble in the marriage, nor that her husband had been cheating on her. She had been so wrapped up in herself, that she had not seen the warning signs.

Celia was grief stricken and was unable to fully cope for the next ten years of her life. She leaned heavily on her teen-aged children who, in a way brought themselves up most of the time and looked after her needs, as well as their own.

Her children loved her, but because she seldom gave them any guidance and was prone to complaining, her children lost respect for her. Her youngest son Bill drifted through life doing as little as possible around the home and simply put in time at school.

Five years after her husband left her, Celia realised that financially she would have to work, so applied for a part-time position as receptionist. Her hours of employment were unusual because she worked from six till ten in the morning. Because of these early hours of work, she found she had to cut her evenings short and was often in bed before nine o'clock. She seldom dated for two reasons. She still couldn't forget her husband and the thought of having an affair or being intimate with another man went against her beliefs as a strong Roman Catholic.

One of her friends introduced her to a man called Albert. The two of them hit it off right away. Both were racquetball lovers, liked quiet evenings at home and hit it off right away. This friendship continued for several years. Albert wanted Celia to marry him, but she kept putting him off refusing to make a commitment. She confided in her female friends that she felt that the magic was missing in their relationship and that he was too unsophisticated. They eventually broke up. Celia then spent her time working, visiting her grown children and female friends.

Celia had extreme mood swings. She could be on top of the world one hour and in the depths of despair the next. Her depressions were so severe that they influenced everything she did. She spent most of her energy railing over how her life had been. Most of her sentences began with the statements, *'If only...'* Or *'I should have...'* Or *'Why didn't I do something with my life earlier.'*

One of her friends is a trained counsellor who tried desperately to help Celia solve her problems and change her negative attitude into a positive one.

For some reason Celia surrounded herself with positive-thinking friends, who tried their best to convince Celia that it wasn't too late to try something new. Unfortunately, Celia kept comparing her life to that of her successful female friends who were high achievers and set reasonable goals for themselves. She insisted that others were more important than she and related her own lack of fulfilment to something outside herself. She didn't understand that there's nothing wrong with appreciating others' accomplishments. But it did become a problem when she modelled her behaviour on their standards, not her own.

Celia learned how to set goals for herself, but normally stopped trying before she achieved them. She always had a reason for quitting. It's unlikely that Celia will change her way of living unless she receives professional counselling. Her friends hope that she will do this for herself. In the meantime, her friend's patience at her inactivity towards helping herself, is alienating her from their strength.

Celia will likely lose her positive-thinking friends soon unless she changes her approach to life, which in turn will likely make her even more depressed.

Remembering the past can be a painful, counterproductive occasion. Using twenty-twenty hindsight, you can probably see exactly where you went wrong - on a job interview, in a love relationship or in moving to a new city. These thoughts can cause immobility and make a person remain in the negative rut they're in. They feel depressed, uneasy and even out of control of their life. If this sounds familiar, you've probably fallen into this trap. This kind of thinking has become a habit, but habits can change. In this case it will take more than a little effort, but you can do it!

Try to stop thinking of life in black or white terms. There are many grey areas in between. Some feel that if they fail at something, that they're a failure as a person. Others are perfectionists who believe that if they don't perform flawlessly, they'll disgrace themselves. Many set complex goals that would be impossible to reach. Because it's impossible to be perfect, they're always dissatisfied with themselves.

Others give up too soon. At the first sign of trouble, they convince themselves that they weren't meant to succeed at something. Instead of trying another avenue or another way of doing something, they quit trying. Many pass the buck, stating something or someone made them fail. By blaming others for their failure, they feel they can absolve themselves of its responsibility. Many make a mountain out of a molehill and magnify the expected results of making a mistake. If a real calamity were to happen - they give up completely.

These people are constantly comparing themselves to others. They compare their successes, status and position to others. They believe that people like others more than them - anything they feel puts them in a lower category than their associates. Others are always happier, more famous and more successful, worth more. Others' successes only made this person more depressed at their own status in life.

These people accept criticism as always being true. Not only do they accept criticism from others willingly, but they're also the ones who criticise everything they do themselves as well. The little voice in their head is always ridiculing them about their perceived failures. They punish themselves with statements such as *'I should have known that was going to happen. Where were my brains?'*

They jump to conclusions without knowing all the facts and assume they know what others are thinking. On the other hand, they assume others know exactly how they're feeling as well. They should communicate with others so they can confirm their beliefs.

CHAPTER FOUR
BEING CREATIVE

Rehearsals

If you need to explain your decision-making ideas to others, it's a good idea to rehearse the situation with an unbiased person who will play the *"devil's advocate"* to come up with objections to your ideas. This will ensure that you are ready for any resistance to your proposed decision. Be creative in handling their resistance. If no one else is available to assist with this:

Make your presentation in front of a mirror. Do you appear hostile, passive, aggressive? Are others likely to listen to your ideas? If not, adjust your wording so they are more likely to cooperate.

Make a tape recording of what you want to say and edit until you have it memorised.

Using Creativity in problem-solving:

We're all born full of creativity. Criticism of our behaviour slowly but surely stops this creativity and affects our self-image. Then at school, children are encouraged to become clones - to fit in - to lose their individuality, which stifles creativity even more. Those that do not conform receive labels like: *"radical, wave-makers, extremist, militant, fanatical, rebellious, revolutionary or different."*

We use our right brain for our creative ideas. This includes visual memory (remembers the face, but not the name) artistic talent and creativity. Our left side does the analytical thinking that relates to language and logic.

We're split in half - one half keeps us safe (the safekeeping self) and the other is the part that yearns for everything (our experimental self). These segments are often at war with each other. Without both of these areas functioning - we're handicapped.

Brainstorming was a tool devised to assist in creative problem solving. Initially, most of those who used the technique were men. This technique proved moderately successful until a manager couldn't make it to a meeting, so sent his secretary to take notes for him. Since everyone had to participate, she contributed as well. The managers couldn't believe the outcome - she came up with two of the four workable suggestions. They couldn't understand why her answers were better than those of professionals who understood all aspects of the problem.

At the next meeting, they tried an experiment. All the managers brought their secretaries to the meeting. Most of the ideas again came from the women! The women didn't censor their own ideas as critically as the men. Before speaking, most men generally examined their ideas to see if they are *"good enough"* before submitting them to the group. Some did this out of a fear of looking silly and some because they couldn't turn off the self-censoring mechanism that told them, *"That won't work."*

In this case, the women were instructed to let ideas flow unrestricted - so they did. They suggested any idea they could think of. It didn't matter whether it was a good idea, because they knew their suggestions would be evaluated after the brainstorming session.

If the men had practiced listening to their *"gut reactions"* the way the women listened to their *"intuitions"* they wouldn't have had this problem. Many businesses now make sure half the participants in creative problem-solving sessions are women.

Let your *"little kid"* out and allow your creative juices to flow. You'll be surprised how effective it is - not only thinking up advertising campaigns or marketing a product - but in finding creative solutions to difficult problems. It will allow you to take something that is average and make it superior.

CHAPTER FIVE

TRAINING DECISIONS

We'll now go on to solving another problem - that of adequately training your staff so they can do a good job for you.

Qualities of a good trainer:

Trainers need many qualities to be successful. Some of these qualities are used by those researching and preparing seminars. For instance:

1. Good research ability.

2. Attention to detail.

3. Ability to determine training needs.

4. Ability to prepare a seminar to meet those training needs.

5. Ability to sift through research material and take out only what is applicable.

6. Good knowledge of training methods.

7. Good sense of timing - able to time segments to keep learners' interest.

8. Ability to prepare interesting sessions with variety and different methods of presenting material; and

9. Well organised.

Those who present seminars require the following qualities:

1. Interested in people.

2. Like dealing with people.

3. Knowledge of the subject being taught.

4. Good verbal and presentation skills.

5. Self-assured.

6. Well organised.

7. Empathetic to others.

8. Good listener.

9. Ability to *"bring out"* quiet participants.

10. Ability to create an atmosphere of learning.

11. Does not threaten participants.

12. *"In tune"* with the mood of the group.

13. Ability to explain information and skill knowledge in a clear, concise manner that is clearly understood by the participants.

14. Ability to read others' body language.

15. Ability to *"ad lib."*

16. Sense of humour.

17. Adaptable.

18. Perceptive.

19. Patient.

20. Radiates confidence.

21. Punctual, prepared and professional.

22. Good physical appearance; and

23. High energy level.

#21 is crucial to the success of a presenter. It's unforgivable for a trainer to be late for a session. If they're not properly prepared - all they do is waste everyone's time. If they don't conduct themselves professionally, they won't gain the respect of the audience, nullifying the content of the training session. Many adult learners would simply leave the session.

Teaching Adults:

As people grow older, it becomes more and more difficult to change established behaviour. Society has often encouraged people to be closed-minded towards new ideas. The creativity curve in most children levels off between six and eight years of age. This is when society dumps more negative criticism on children than positive. Therefore, when they become adults, they're often much more comfortable with negative criticism than with praise. They're used to feeling bad, rather than good about themselves.

If you've been trained as a teacher of children, you'll likely *"bomb"* at teaching adults, because an entirely different approach is necessary. Adults feel that this type of instructor *"talks down to them."* Teachers would be more in tune and perceptive if they treated child learners in this manner as well. Children respond better if they're treated as if they were *"little adults."*

As trainers, your major responsibility may be to overcome the negative feelings your participants obtained in school as a child. This is accomplished by providing an atmosphere conducive to learning with low-risk factors for the individuals.

Many people resist taking responsibility for their actions and their own futures. The book *"The Cinderella Complex"* by Collette Dowling describes this phenomenon in some women. It explains how many women, live their lives under the assumption that someone else will look after them. Therefore, they have difficulty making any decision without getting the advice of at least one other person. They resist taking responsibility for their actions and therefore their futures as well.

As a trainer, you'll need to overcome this obstacle. Men, too, may drift into this. They let the *"organisation"* or *"Big Brother"* make all their work decisions for them - to determine their career paths. They float through life, making few direct decisions for themselves.

Our present social system heavily encourages dependence, conformity, submission and role-playing as the norm. Others follow their urges and grow, take risks, change and take charge of their lives and destiny. Sometimes, though, this growth and change can be painful.

For instance, an employee attends a workshop on *"Interpersonal Skills"* - returns to work but run into difficulties. S/he's anxious to use his/her new skills but finds his/her co-workers and supervisor sceptical of his/her actions. Often s/he's forced to revert to his/her old pattern (even if it was a bad one) so s/he doesn't *"make waves."* Follow-up sessions will enable trainers to see whether participants were able to use the skills effectively in their work environment.

As instructors, you'll need to be in tune with the objectives of the group - be able to motivate them to learn the necessary information and new skills. It takes a certain kind of person to do this.

Giving training as a *"reward or a perk"* for good performance or because Derrick hasn't had any training this year; are poor reasons for sending anyone to training sessions. Training should be for specific reasons only.

Try to make sure attendees are there because they desire and need the training being offered. It's a good idea to determine the driving and restraining forces that might be in place for the trainees. One restraining force to learning might be a heavy workload that's piling up while they attend the training. Try to have someone take over their duties while they're away so they can concentrate on the training.

Determine at the beginning of the session why each of them feels the training session they're at will benefit them (learner's objectives). You might find out as I did that half the participants of an in-house training program were there under duress. Some may not have known they were to attend the seminar until the day before the session started.

If you need to face this kind of situation, say, *"I know some of you are here under duress and didn't ask for this training. I'd like you to decide whether you're going to put in time here at this session or are you going to fool them and learn something?"* I tried this and was surprised by the positive results. I had given the choice back to the participants. They now could choose what their attention level would be during the seminar. Most decided to *"fool them and learn something."*

Characteristics of adult learners:

In general, there are certain characteristics that distinguish adult learners from child learners.

1. Most adults are highly motivated to learn as long as it applies to their needs.

2. Adults like to take part in determining their own training needs.

3. Adults like sequential learning, with graduated stages of learning - lots of feedback and re-enforcement from their trainer.

4. Adults enjoy novelty in learning - but can be *"turned off"* or frightened by some ideas if they're too far out.

5. Adults have difficulty being re-trained; have set ideas on how to do things. Trainers need to show them why the new idea or method is superior to the old one.

6. An authoritarian set-up for learning is not acceptable and often increases the risk factor.

7. Learning will be retained if it's used as soon as possible.

8. Adults have set patterns of behaviour - this pattern must be *"unset"* so learning can take place.

9. Adults usually require a longer time to *"lock-in"* and do tasks a different way.

10. Adults are less tolerant of *"busy work"* which doesn't have immediate or direct application to their own objectives.

11. The older adult may have restricted powers of adjustment to external forces and distractions. They require more constant and ideal environmental conditions to learn or work efficiently.

12. Because adult learners are typically evening or after work students, they're more likely to be physically and mentally tired. This makes them less alert when coming

to class. This, however, is offset by their increased desire to learn.

13. Adults have more experience in living, which gives them the advantage of being more readily able to relate new facts to experience.

14. Training is mainly a voluntary decision for them, and their attendance often represents a considerable sacrifice. Having made this important and commendable decision, they expect (and deserve) the trainer's respect and to be treated as adult learners.

Differences in adult and child learners:

1. Adults are more realistic. They've lived longer and have a different perspective of life. They no longer see life through rose-coloured glasses, but as a set of realities.

2. Adults have had more experience. They have insights and see relationships not discerned by children. They've accumulated wisdom that gives them a sense of what's likely to work and what's not.

3. Adults have needs that are more concrete and immediate than those of children. They're impatient with long discourses on theory and like to see theory applied with practical solutions.

4. Adults are not a captive audience. They attend voluntarily and if their interest is lacking, they're inclined to stop attending.

5. Adults expect to be treated as mature persons and resent having instructors talk down to them.

6. Adults enjoy having their talents and abilities recognised and to be given the opportunity to enhance them during a teaching situation.

7. Adult groups are likely to be more diversified than youth groups. Differences increase with age and mobility. Therefore, adult learners come from a wider variety of backgrounds.

8. Adults, through their fifties and beyond, can learn as well as youth. They may not perform some assignments as rapidly as children because of a slowing up of physical functions.

9. Adults attend classes often with a mixed set of motives - educational, social, recreational and sometimes out of a sense of duty.

10. Adults may be tired when attending classes. They appreciate teaching devices that add interest and liveliness such as variety of methods, audio-visual aids, change of pace or sense of humour.

Learning process:

Learning involves personal change, which each trainee responds to differently. Motivation is the most important factor of learning. People learn what they want to learn, when they want to learn and under what conditions. Keeping up with or ahead of their peer group may be a motivator. It could simply be the need to learn, to keep advancing or to earn more money.

If the conditions of learning are not satisfactory, the training might be a waste of time. These conditions could be:

Room too hot or too cold.

Chairs uncomfortable.

Too much distracting noise;

Lights too bright (usually fluorescent).

Not enough variety in learning.

They're there under duress or pressed for time.

They have a feeling of failure due to the atmosphere or the style of instruction.

The ability to learn has its limitations because of the person's motor skills or level of intellect. A trainee learns best by participating in the learning process. The learner must be able to predict where they will use the learning. Describe similarities in different ways until they recognise and understand the connection of the learning material to their personal situation.

How to "lock-in" training:

Unless verbal data is repeated many times, it will be poorly retained. A combination of verbal and written material is far superior for retention of information by the trainee. Keep in mind that trainees retain:

10% of what they read (handouts, manuals).

20% of what they hear (have explained to them).

30% of what they see done (demonstrations).

40% of what they read and hear.

50% of what they read, hear and see demonstrated.

70% of what they read, hear, see demonstrated and they explain what they will do.

90% of what they read, hear, see demonstrated, they explain what they will do and then demonstrate themselves.

Here's how you can utilise the above information:

1. Trainer gives handout, which shows the steps participants will take to complete the task (10% retention).

2. Trainer explains the information on the handouts (20% retention).

3. When you combine #1 and #2 the retention is 40%

4. Trainer demonstrates to the trainee how to complete the task (30% retention).

5. When you use all three of the above (50% retention).

6. In addition to 5, ask the trainee to use paraphrasing to explain verbally what they're going to do (70% retention).

7. In addition to 5 and 6, trainee demonstrates for the trainer how s/he will complete the task.

This method uses the trainee's sight, hearing and touch senses. It encourages learners to be better listeners. This is because they know that there'll be a test during the training. Give learner written back-up information for future reference and have them use the training as soon as possible.

Recall is another training fundamental. Some may forget the overall training but can recall something they've learned which stimulates more memory of the issues taught in the course. An atmosphere of approval and acceptance where participants can offer ideas and confirm their thought-patterns relating to the issues is essential for true learning.

Refresher training courses re-enforce the original information given but are usually presented in a more capsulated form. One also tends to repeat behaviour that seems to bring rewards and not repeat behaviour that seems to be without reward or to bring punishment.

For example, a test is given, and errors are corrected. Using positive feedback, the trainer would say, *"You had most of it right. This is the only area where you went astray."* Concentrate on what they did right, not what they did wrong!

Determining training needs:

Problems in behaviour or productivity are often eliminated by training. Training needs must be established before writing or implementing any training program. This is normally the job of the researcher or the person preparing the training package or manual. You can determine training needs by or from:

1. Performance appraisals that have a section relating to training needs.
2. Exit interviews - may identify that the employee left because the company didn't meet his/her training needs.
3. Supervisors identify performance problems.
4. Clients - usually in the form of complaints.
5. Organisational requirements - new equipment, policies, procedures or new ways of doing things company-wide.

5. Union requirements.

6. Technological advances - to upgrade employee's knowledge - usually an on-going occurrence in most companies.

7. Recruiters - the gap between qualification of candidates and the requirements of the position.

8. Employees themselves ask for training.

9. Production/work output - problems or new methods determined.

10. Morale problems.

11. Company questionnaires.

12. Accident statistics.

You may have identified the following that have training needs:

a. Individuals for personal upgrading.

b. Group needs (learning how to use a new computer); or

c. Organisation-wide training (such as implementation of a new performance appraisal system).

The employees, themselves must:

Be willing to perform: Resistance can be cultural, personal, an unwillingness to take risks; work environment may not be conducive (the kind of supervision etc.) types of employees or general work attitudes. The supervisor's or manager's attitude controls seventy-five percent of this area.

Can perform: Correct this by offering proper training. Make sure the training is offered to both men and women.

Have the Opportunity: Could be self-generated (employee asks for the opportunity) or their supervisor offers it for developmental purposes or through necessity for the employee to stay on the job.

CHAPTER SIX

TRAINING OF SUPERVISORS

Upper management might believe that there are behaviour or production problems in a supervisor or manager. The supervisor who finds that s/he is constantly describing his/her staff as *"second rate"* is likely describing his/her own performance. This supervisor's not providing the proper training guidelines and motivation for co-operation of his/her employees. Many of these supervisors haven't had the basic training required to do their own jobs properly. Or it's possible their manager didn't have the basic training required to get the job done.

Supervisors have the responsibility of not only delegating work, checking work, etc., but to:

a. Identify training needs.

b. Provide on-the-job training.

c. Help develop training programs; and

d. Take part in training to meet the needs of any new policy or technology that affects his/her staff.

Companies must keep up with technology and how businesses are run. Unfortunately, the people at the top of the hierarchy often cause difficulties that the underlings would like to change.

Who do you think causes the most trouble and are the most difficult people to deal with in the workplace? Is it clients, colleagues, subordinates or *"the boss?"*

When I first started offering my *"Dealing with Difficult People"* seminars, I assumed that *"off the wall"* clients would be the most difficult group to deal with in the workplace. My second guess - was difficult clients, then colleagues. I was wrong in making those assumptions. My research has proven (confirmed by the more than 55,000 participants of my seminars) that the most difficult people faced by those in the workplace are not clients, colleagues or subordinates - but overwhelmingly, the employees' supervisors or managers!

Why is this the case? Because many Human Resources and Training Managers are failing when it comes to providing adequate supervisory training to staff who are responsible for the completion of work by others.

Even though these people have titles such as: supervisor, foreman/woman, manager, superintendent, department head, vice president, or even C.E.O., most have not received the basic training necessary to enable them to successfully supervise others.

What are the qualities of a good supervisor/manager?

Communicates well

Good delegator, motivator

Flexible, fair and consistent

Good time manager - is organised

Patient and foresighted

Keeps employees informed

Good trainer

Approachable and available

Open to new ideas

Uses positive reinforcement

Gives constructive discipline

Encouraging of others

Good leader, problem solver

Comfortable with power

Can pace themselves

Dresses the part

Empathetic and tactful

Self-controlled

Assertive & knowledgeable

Good role model

Accepts responsibility

Sense of humour

Team player

Honest and trustworthy

Guides rather than bosses

Gives credit where it's due

Positive image

Keep confidences

What is a Supervisor/Manager's major responsibility?

A supervisor's major responsibility is to provide his or her staff with all the tools that are necessary for them to do a good job.

What is an Employee's major responsibility?

An employee's major responsibility is to make his or her supervisor look good!

It's possible that the person supervising or managing others has been identified as a:

Supervisor or Manager from hell!

What do they do that causes so much distress to their staff? These difficult supervisors (I use the word supervisor - but this includes all the above titles) make mistakes such as:

Discipline their staff in front of workmates or clients.

This is an example of bullying so, before you do anything about this situation, prepare yourself for the eventuality that things might get worse before they get better. Check your company policies and procedures manuals to learn how bullying is handled in your company. Document what happened to you and when it happened.

Talk privately with your supervisor using feedback to let him or her know how the behaviour has affected you.

Say, *"I have a problem, and I need your help in solving it. I'd like to talk to you about something that's affecting my productivity. Last week you disciplined me in front of clients and colleagues. I found this very demoralising and embarrassing. I'd like to request that if you need to correct my behaviour in the future, that you do so in private, where your comments won't be overheard."* Then show him/her the company policy relating to bullying.

Harass staff (through bullying or sexual harassment).

Bullying is a learned behaviour and unless it's stopped when they're children, this behaviour can become a way of life. Bullying at any level is a play on power and is unacceptable everywhere in society. And when the victim complains about the bullying, they're often labelled a *"woos"* or a *"sissy"* by the bully. How dare these bullies try to make their victims feel guilty, when they're the ones who are in the wrong! Bullies are cowards who don't play fair. They use their power (be it perceived or real) to lord it over others and desperately need anger management.

Unfortunately, in Australia the bullying laws are still in their infancy and there is little legal protection for workers. If workers do take the bully to court, they face hefty legal bills with no assurance that they will be reimbursed for those expenses. Many just throw up their hands, leave the company and learn from the experience - and the bully gets off again. This is the new millennium and yet some companies are still operating with cavemen/women mentalities. I've witnessed bullying in the workplace so often that I've come to believe that this draconian style of behaviour is not only tolerated, but seems to be the norm, rather than the exception in Australian companies. But is that any excuse for not stopping this unacceptable behaviour?

Be sure to check the bullying laws where you live.

Some companies have policies on how to deal with bullying but don't follow-through and protect their workers against it. Hence the employee is forced to take it to court.

Victorian laws are making a stab at dealing with this unacceptable behaviour, but these changes fall short of the mark by insisting that bullying must be repetitive and ongoing. To the victim - one incident of bullying is enough and should have all the protection of the law to deal with it. There should be zero tolerance to bullying - by society, companies and the law.

However, there is hope. As this book is written many Australian States are in the process of up-to-dating laws relating to this corporate disgrace. Those who have been bullied will need to lobby ruthlessly to ensure that proper protection is put in place for themselves and future workers.

If you've already talked to your boss about how repulsed you are by his/her bullying, and nothing has changed - you have no choice but to go over his/her head. However, be prepared - because even his/her superiors might do nothing to stop the bullying. You may have to leave your employment and look for work elsewhere (with no guarantee that you won't run into it in the new company). The other alternative is to prepare for a lengthy and costly legal battle in the courts. It's your choice.

Organisations have a responsibility to ensure the workplace is free from harassment. Sexual harassment is a term covering unwelcome sexual behaviour and is unlawful, direct discrimination on the ground of sex. Co-workers, as well as superiors may be responsible and charged for acts of sexual harassment.

A complaint of sexual harassment does not necessarily mean that sexual harassment has taken place. Organisations have been charged with reverse discrimination. This happens when employees don't receive merited promotions and bonuses. Instead, a workmate receives them in return for sexual favours given to a supervisor.

No longer can others in positions of power *"look the other way"* and ignore that sexual harassment is occurring. For instance, if I'm a supervisor and do nothing when I see another person sexually harassing an employee, it's believed that I've condoned the action. If the employee knows that I saw or know about the situation and did nothing, s/he can charge both the offender and the witnessing supervisor (me) with sexual harassment.

Each incident may be relatively minor, but if continued over a prolonged period, can be very stressful to the victim. Harassment can produce a hostile work environment that can adversely affect the terms and conditions of employment and make it impossible for the person to continue employment. Sexual harassment amounts to unlawful sex discrimination if an employee is obliged to continue to work in an environment which is generally hostile demeaning or intimidating.

In Australia, it's been established that most sex discrimination is against women. An employer has a legal responsibility to ensure that there are no policies or practices operating within an organisation that directly or indirectly discriminate against women. An employer can be vicariously liable for the actions of an employee even if the employer was unaware of the actual actions of the employee. If your company doesn't have a sexual harassment policy - insist that they prepare one and make it available to all staff members. Many companies have sexual harassment advisors.

Research shows that seventy to eighty per cent of women have experienced one or more forms of sexual harassment while working. Fifty-two per cent of them lost a job because of it. This is criminal and needs swift action to eliminate such future harassment.

It's important to take steps to prevent sexual harassment in the workplace. Line management needs information about what harassment is, and how to receive, investigate and resolve complaints. It's also essential that managers are aware of their responsibilities and the organisation's policy on sexual harassment.

If you believe you have been sexually harassed, it's up to you to check your State Harassment laws. Should you be the object of sexual harassment you should:

1. Tell the person that you object to whatever s/he's doing or saying. *Let him or her know you really mean it!* If necessary, explain that his/her behaviour is a form of sexual harassment, and you expect it to stop immediately. Record everything that happens - date, time, events, witnesses, etc. Recognise that you're probably not the only one who's been sexually harassed by this person. Find out if there are others so you can lodge a group complaint.

2. If the person does the same thing (or something similar) again, repeat your earlier objections. Back this up with a written letter or email. Relate to your earlier verbal complaints. State only the facts, not assumptions. Make at least four copies of this information.

   -- Send one copy to the offending person

   -- Keep one copy for your records

   -- One to his or her supervisor, your supervisor, (and the Chief Executive Officer of your company, if you think it's appropriate).

3. If the behaviour continues, or the company or union has not dealt with it, lodge a formal complaint with your local Equal Employment Opportunities Commission. When in doubt, call your local E.E.O. office and talk to a trained counsellor. If the situation involves physical assault, involve the police by lodging a sexual assault charge.

   Note: If the first incident is serious enough, object verbally, send a letter or email (with copies to applicable parties) and lodge a formal complaint with the Equal Employment Opportunities Commission.)

Have temper tantrums.

This is an example of workplace bullying. One manager realised that he had hired a supervisor who had problems dealing with anger and had violent temper tantrums. Someone slipped up when conducting reference checks on the employee. This employee is using aggressive behaviour and is misusing his position of power. He has likely been doing this in his past positions as well. If you allow his behaviour to continue - you are setting your company up for a bullying or harassment charge so you must stop his behaviour - now.

Adults who still resort to temper tantrums to get their way, haven't grown up. They use tantrums, because they've learned that they get what they want if they yell and carry on. They often lack the communication skills that enable them to use tact and diplomacy to get work done through their employees. They love the control they have over others and enjoy watching everyone jump to do their bidding. Most of them desperately need anger management counselling.

Don't wait for the next explosive episode to erupt. Call him into your office and confront him with your knowledge about his behaviour. Use facts. Relate exactly what you witnessed and heard. Then relate the repercussions his behaviour caused not only to his co-workers and staff, but to your clients who may have been within earshot. Ask him to explain why he acted the way he did.

Explain that you feel he's abusing his position of power and that his behaviour is a form of bullying and harassment. His actions are so serious that you'll be putting a written warning on his file. Recommend that he obtain counselling on how to handle his anger. Be clear about the consequences should he repeat his destructive behaviour.

There can be a positive element to this kind of dialogue. Your confrontation about his actions could start a dialogue that will make him see how destructive his behaviour is, not only to his career aspirations, but to his relationship with others as well.

If he uses this type of behaviour again, follow through with your consequences. This type of behaviour usually warrants one or two written warnings, then the person is usually terminated. Along the way it's essential that you keep detailed, factual documentation of what transpired in case he decides to take you to court and charge your company with wrongful dismissal. Learn more about this in Chapter 12.

Don't try to stop him/her in mid-stream of his tantrum. Simply listen and force yourself not to be affected by the anger and frustration s/he's trying to thrust upon you. When s/he finally finishes his/her tirade say, *"I can see you're angry about this. Why don't I give you a chance to calm down – then we can discuss this issue?"* Then walk away. If s/he continues to behave in this manner say, *"I'm very uncomfortable being around you when you're out of control. This is unacceptable behaviour and is a form of harassment and bullying. When you've calmed down, I'll be glad to discuss this rationally with you."*

Make sure you document each incident where his behaviour is unacceptable (having a witness helps) and either go to his superior or to your Human Resources representative to initiate charges of harassment.

Are moody - have unpredictable behaviour.

Most moody people are very immature, have low self-esteem and many feel they must take every affront personally. Follow above instructions and start documenting his/her behaviour in case you decide to take further action.

Label their staff's behaviour (stupid, dumb) or make sarcastic remarks, instead of trying to correct the actual behaviour of the staff member.

The boss who labels employees (rather than dealing with their behaviour) is bound to de-motivate his or her staff. Talk to your supervisor privately. Say, *"I have a problem, and I need your help in solving it. On my performance appraisal, you put down that you didn't like my attitude, but when I asked for specifics, you refused to give them to me. And the last few times you've corrected my work you've said that I was 'stupid' and 'dumb.' I'm upset that you've given me those labels and I don't know how to improve my performance or what you really want from me.*

I'd like to go back to the comment from my performance appraisal about my attitude. What did I do wrong that you objected to?"

Her supervisor replied, *"Well, you were rude to Mrs. Brown."* (Rude is another label that does not discuss her behaviour.)

"What specifically did I say to Mrs. Brown that was rude?"

"You told her that you had better things to do with your time other than listen to her constant complaints."

Now the employee knows what is wrong with her *"attitude"* and can change her behaviour accordingly.

The employee did the same with the other two labels and was able to determine the exact behaviour that was not suitable. Only then did she have something she could deal with and change.

At a later meeting with her supervisor where he complimented her on a task well done, she replied, *"Thanks for the compliment. I must admit that I'm so used to hearing about the things I do wrong that it's a pleasure to receive confirmation about the things I've done right."*

Don't value or respect others' opinions (especially their subordinates).

Don't give recognition for a job well done. Instead of concentrating on the 98 per cent their staff do right, they concentrate on the two per cent they do incorrectly.

Don't back up their staff when dealing with customer complaints. (The customer complains but instead of backing their staff, they commiserate with the client and don't give their employee the opportunity to defend his or her side of the story.)

When your supervisor receives a client complaint, the first thing s/he should say to the client is, *"Let me investigate this and I'll get back to you."* The supervisor mediates between what the client believes and what the staff member believes and come to a compromise or solution. Both the supervisor and the employee must understand that if the staff member caused the problem - the client deserves TLC (tender loving care) in the form of extra services or action. If the employee is right, the supervisor must defend his/her side of the issue and explain to the client what they *can* do about solving his/her complaint. This often involves suggesting two or three alternatives that will solve the client's problem.

Don't provide an adequate up-to-date job description with key performance indicators (KPIs) and standards of performance for the tasks performed to achieve those KPIs. Please see information shown in Chapter 2 to learn more about this.

Use the following to convince your company why the above type of position description is essential for the smooth running of the company:

1. It's an excellent training tool to compare an employee's capabilities against those required by the position allowing the company to determine the required training to fill that gap.

2. It's the primary tool to determine qualifications for recruiting new employees.

3. Many government training grants to companies require a detailed job description so they can determine what is required of employees compared to their present level of knowledge and ability.

4. Both employee and employer know exactly what the employee is to do, and the employee's performance can be measured against clear written objectives.

5. Duties do not *"fall through the cracks"* and eliminates the expression, *"I didn't know I was responsible for that!"*

6. Morale of employees normally rises 100% when it's clear what their employers expect from them.

When job descriptions are completed properly, company performance appraisals will be based on objective, rather than subjective measures. There are no surprises at performance appraisal time, because it's clear to both the employee and their supervisor exactly what is expected of the employee.

Should the employee be terminated, the employer can show exactly what standards of performance were not met by the employee and the documentation to prove that the employee had an opportunity to improve his or her behaviour or performance.

It's a vital tool for manpower planning that helps determine the gaps between the employees' skills and abilities and those required to fill their next promotional position.

Hire the wrong staff

If recruiters, supervisors and managers don't take enough time when hiring employees, they'll find they've set themselves up for a period of misery. Problems can occur if:

1. The right questions aren't asked on the interview.

2. The interviewers aren't knowledgeable enough to hire competent personnel; and

3. References aren't checked properly.

Companies may end up with a real loser, who, instead of helping their company with production, cause more work in the long run. Have you hired someone to learn that:

a) They lied on the interview about how long they'd worked for a company.

b) They told you they had more experience than they had.

c) They didn't fit in with the existing staff.

d) They were not able to handle the duties of the position after considerable in-house or professional training.

e) Their work ethic left much to be desired.

f) YOU were on a different wavelength than they and found it difficult to get them to do things your way.

g) You required a self-starter, and the employee requires very detailed instructions to get anything done.

h) You find the person who was hired to work on the front lines dealing directly with clients, doesn't have the people-skills you require.

(i) The person has a negative attitude, who gripes and complains about everything which eventually affects his/her co-workers resulting in low morale for all your staff.

j) Your company has installed a new computer system, but the new employee is unwilling or unable to pick up the new technology.

k) The person looked very presentable on the interview, but their day-to-day appearance leaves much to be desired even after several talks you've had with him/her.

l) The person puts things off so long (procrastinates) that project deadlines aren't met.

m) The employee is a perfectionist in everything they do, which holds up progress.

n) Employee is a know-it-all, doesn't follow directions, does things his/her own way and bucks the system.

I'm sure you've run into the above kinds of employees in your daily work situation. It's hard to evaluate people's ability to fit the needs of a position. Unless you've had years of experience, it can be a very intimidating experience. Proper interviewing, screening and especially reference checking of the above employees would have eliminated most of these problems. So, doing things correctly *before* they're hired is crucial. If this requires Recruitment

Techniques training on your part - make sure you obtain it, so you don't hire another *"dud."*

Reference Checking

The following information should be included on company employment application forms that will protect companies from being charged under the privacy act:

I certify that the statements made by me in this application are true and complete. I understand and agree that a false statement may disqualify me from employment or result in dismissal.

Permission is granted for (your company name) to contact my past employers for references.

Date _____

Signature _____

When conducting reference checks, start with the last supervisor / manager and work backwards chronologically. Contact at least two, preferably three former managers. It's best to speak with the applicant's former managers rather than someone in the former company's Human Resources Department.

Don't provide the necessary training to fill the gap between the job requirements and the employee's skills.

Many organisations offer a variety of on-the-job training for their employees, but frequently, women are denied access to these training courses. Their managers make incorrect or stereotypical assumptions about the working patterns of women and the number of years women intend to remain in the workforce. These assumptions are applied to all female employees - regardless of the actual job performance or career ambitions of individual women. Consequently, the organisation may not provide the information or facilities for these women to participate in training programs.

Your first step is to establish an Affirmative Action Program in your organisation. Contact the EEO (Equal

Employment Opportunities) representatives in your area to assist in setting up such a program. This program will assess the skills, qualifications and ambitions of women employees so their training needs are realistically identified and will outline the employer's responsibility in providing equitable training opportunities for both male and female employees.

In assessing the training opportunities for women within the organisation, the following factors should be examined:

1. How is information on internal training courses made available throughout the organisation?

2. Is information on the content of the training courses and the potential benefit it may provide to the career path of individual employees easily available to all employees?

3. Are supervisors or others who are responsible for the selection of employees to attend training courses fully aware of the organisations' Affirmative Action program and the need to fully utilise all the talents and skills available to the organisation?

4. Are all employees actively encouraged by management to use all opportunities for training and development when they arise?

5. Are training courses conducted in convenient locations to ensure that employees with childcare or domestic responsibilities are not automatically precluded from nomination and selection?

6. Are employees encouraged to self-nominate for courses that they believe will be of benefit to their job opportunities, rather than waiting for supervisors to nominate them?

Conduct performance appraisals on staff without a proper job description upon which to base their evaluation.

If staff members don't know what's expected of them, and neither does the supervisor - how do supervisors have the audacity to attempt an evaluation on how well their employees performed their duties?

How often should performance appraisals be conducted? There's quite a bit of flexibility here, depending upon the needs of the position. The recommended times are:

1. Shortly after the employee is hired, the first part of the probationary performance appraisal (which lists the expectations) is completed.

2. Two weeks *before* the employee's probationary performance appraisal period is over - the performance appraisal meeting is held. This is the time when the supervisor decides whether the employee will be accepted by the company as a permanent employee.

3. If the employee is accepted as a permanent employee, a new performance appraisal is started for the next evaluation period.

There are two methods of determining the employee's yearly performance appraisal thereafter:

1. It can be held on the anniversary date of when the employee started with the company; or

2. Could be held once a year at the same time for all employees.

Some companies have bi-yearly performance appraisals. Many companies do performance appraisals before and after every special project the staff member completes regardless of the time frame of the project. The company must decide which method is best to meet their staff's individual needs.

Performance appraisal systems that evaluate such subjective things as:

judgment,

initiative,

attitude, or

interpersonal skills

are not fair appraisal systems and should be replaced.

There are many advantages of doing regular performance appraisals:

Putting things down on paper makes people more specific about what they expect.

It allows the staff member to take part in setting standards they feel they can meet.

Makes people more productive and motivated to do a good job.

New ideas and methods for completing tasks can be discussed and encouraged.

Keeps people from being buried or lost in the system.

The *"good guys"* or high achievers don't get passed over.

The *"bad guys"* or low achievers and those using unacceptable behaviour, don't get to hide.

They improve communication between supervisor and staff members. The more the employee is involved in setting his or her own standards, the more likely s/he will react positively.

Employees are often their own worst critics, so should not be allowed to set unrealistic standards of performance.

If the employee doesn't measure up – s/he knows s/he's failed <u>before</u> review date. There are no surprises at performance appraisal time.

Use the same leadership style on all staff members, even though a different leadership style is required.

Leadership:

"Is inspiring people to put forth their best effort."

John F. Kennedy

There are many leadership styles in management - each suitable for different situations and personalities. Some employees need lots of *"rope"* and loose supervision.

Possibly their supervisor is leading them with a style that's more suitable to someone who has an absolute need to know exactly what steps s/he needs to take to accomplish a task. Let your boss know the kind of leadership you need.

You might start by saying, *"I'd like more freedom when accomplishing my tasks. I'm a creative person and usually can visualise what you want and will ask questions to clarify my picture of that. I'm uncomfortable with step-by-step instructions - and like to use my own resources to do tasks. Would you feel comfortable giving me that leeway?"*

Other employees may not feel comfortable unless they receive detailed instructions on how to complete tasks. They usually love routine and are knocked off-balance when changes occur. You on the other hand, love variety and will seldom do a task the same way twice. You're probably entrepreneurial and can see all kinds of ways things can be improved. If your employer doesn't allow you to use your creative juices, you'll likely go elsewhere.

Theory X and Theory Y

Leadership styles differ from highly authoritarian (Theory X) to highly employee participative (Theory Y).

Here are the differences between the two following theories:

Theory Y Assumption 1: People are naturally active; they set goals and enjoy striving.

Theory X Assumptions: People are naturally lazy. They prefer to do nothing.

Theory Y Assumption 2: People seek many satisfactions in work, pride in achievement, enjoyment of process, sense of contribution, pleasure in association and new challenges.

Theory X Assumptions: People work mostly for money, status and rewards.

Theory Y Assumption 3: The main force keeping people productive in their work is the desire to achieve their personal and social goals.

Theory X Assumptions: The main force keeping people productive in their work is fear of being demoted or fired.

Theory Y Assumption 4: People normally mature beyond childhood. They aspire to independence, self-fulfilment and responsibility.

Theory X Assumptions: People remain children grown larger – they're naturally dependent on leaders.

Theory Y Assumption 5: People close to the situation see and feel what is needed and are capable of self-direction

Theory X Assumptions: People expect and depend on direction from above. Don't want to think for themselves.

Theory Y Assumption 6: People who understand and care about what they're doing can devise and improve their own methods of doing work.

Theory X Assumptions: People need to be told, shown and trained in proper methods of work.

Theory Y Assumption 7: People need a sense that they're respected as capable of assuming responsibility and self-direction.

Theory X Assumptions: People need supervisors who will watch them closely enough to be able to praise good work and correct errors.

Theory Y Assumption 8: People seek to give meaning to their lives by identifying with nations, communities, churches, unions, companies and causes.

Theory X Assumptions: People have little concern beyond their immediate material interests.

Theory Y Assumption 9: People need ever-increasing understanding. They need to know why they're doing what they're doing and how it fits in with the company's objectives.

Theory X Assumptions: People need specific instruction on what to do and how to do it. Larger policy issues are none of their business.

Theory Y Assumption 10: People crave genuine respect from their fellow man.

Theory X Assumptions: Pay people well and they'll be happy.

Theory Y Assumption 11: People are naturally integrated. When work and play are too sharply separated, both deteriorate.

Theory X Assumptions: People are naturally compartmentalised. Work demands are entirely different from leisure activities.

Theory Y Assumption 12: People naturally tire of monotonous routine and enjoy new experiences. To some degree, everyone is creative.

Theory X Assumptions: People naturally resist change. They prefer to stay in the old ruts.

Most leadership styles have changed from authoritarian to participative in the last century because:

Changing social values. The class system of the 19th century meant there were large social and business gaps between management and workers. It was seldom possible for a worker to obtain a managerial position unless something unusual happened.

Legislation protecting workers' rights. No longer are 10-year-olds expected to put in 16-hour days. Employees have regular coffee and lunch breaks. Employees now have vacation and statutory holidays, etc.

Supply and demand on the labour market. Mass production of items and diversification of products has meant there are more jobs with more qualifications required, which lessens the gap between workers and management.

Competition - both domestic and foreign. The availability of communication and travel between countries has made it possible for international trade. This increased competition within countries as well.

Declining profit margins. In the early 1900s, it was not unheard of to obtain 30% profit for a product or service because there were few middlemen. Now there are many middlemen involved, rather than the producer selling directly to the consumer.

Profit margins are lower because of mass-production of articles through the availability of automation and robotics. Competition with international markets has caused profit margins to remain low.

Higher level of formal education of workers and management. The gap between workers and management has lessened because there are more intermediary levels between the two extremes. Most free world populations believe that anyone can achieve the level of position they want, if they want it badly enough. They believe the opportunity is available for anyone to become what they want in life providing they have the ability to do so.

Unions and their power. Unions stepped in at the beginning of the last century to fight for the rights of the workers. They were necessary to take employees out of the squalor they often had to work in. On the negative side, unions today are making it almost impossible for some companies to stay in business. This in turn, increases the unemployment level.

Do you find you have to use Theory X on certain employees? For instance, consider #6. Let's say you need to delegate an identical task to two employees. Some employees become very upset if you tell them exactly what steps they're to take to complete an assignment. They're accustomed to receiving assignments and completing them in their own way. They crave variety and new ways of completing tasks.

Other employees are very upset if you don't give them explicit instructions and explain every little detail to them. They're often the same employees who panic if you want them to do something a different way than the way they've done it in the past.

Did you agree with #10 under Theory X assumptions? Do you believe that if you *"Pay people well, they'll be happy?"* For some employees this is true, but most employees can be stimulated to give good performance for a myriad of other reasons.

Did you agree with #11, Theory Y Assumptions? If you look at your friends and acquaintances, you'll find that if they truly enjoy their work, they'll probably do something complementary in their time off. For instance, auto mechanics may spend some of their leisure time looking after their friends' cars. Hairdressers may do their friends' hair and lecturers may offer their services free to non-profit organisations.

Have one set of company rules for staff - another for themselves (do as I say - not do as I do). They bend the rules when clients go over the head of front-line staff, causing embarrassment for staff member.

Rules and regulations of a company <u>must</u> be adhered to by <u>all</u> employees - including supervisors, managers and executives. Talk to your supervisor and go over his/her head if necessary, to confirm company rules and regulations.

Start by speaking to your supervisor, *"I have a problem, and I need your help in solving it. I was upset yesterday after I'd spent half an hour explaining to Mrs. Smith that I couldn't do what she wanted me to do because of a company regulation. As you know, she went over my head to you - and she made a point of letting me know that you let her away with it. Can you imagine how I felt when she made a point of telling me that? I need to know whether this is a rule or not so, I won't have the same thing happen in the future."*

Don't provide policies and procedures or employee handbooks that outline the company rules and regulations for all staff.

Progressive companies not only have detailed policy and procedure manuals, but they provide employee manuals that explain the company rules and regulations to their staff. New employees receive a copy of this manual on their first day of their employment and are encouraged to understand and ask questions about the contents. Many companies have the employee sign a document stating that they have read and understand the information. Then, if they break a company rule or regulation, they can't say *"I didn't know about that rule/regulation!"*

You might suggest to your employer that you take on the task of preparing such an employee manual for your company's employees. You would start with the company policy and procedures manuals and only include the information necessary for employees to understand company rules. This will also encourage your company to update the company policies and procedures as well (this should be done at least annually).

Have poor work ethic.

There are two kinds of supervisors - working supervisors - and those who are solely responsible for delegating tasks to others. If the person's a working supervisor – s/he will likely be doing the same type of tasks as his/her staff, along with his/her supervisory responsibilities.

It may seem as if your boss is not doing his/her share, but if you look behind the scenes - those meetings and reports s/he's preparing are as much work for him/her as yours is for you. And if you do a poor job of completing your tasks, you are not only making yourself look bad but you're making him/her look bad as well. If your performance slips far enough, you will leave him/her no other choice but to reprimand you. Remember - your main function as an employee is to make your boss look good. His/her job is to give you the tools you'll need to allow you to do this.

Do nothing to improve the employee's interest in their jobs (lack of development).

There are two solutions to this problem. Solution One is to prepare for another kind of position where you won't be so bored. Have you had career counselling to determine the kinds of occupations you may be good at? Once you've determined this, take relevant courses in the evenings or take time off and go back to school full-time to gain the ability to enter a new field.

Your employer can supply the second solution. Many use job rotation to keep their employees motivated and happy. All rotated tasks are at the same skill level but involve different tasks. An extra plus for the companies who use job rotation is that this practice keeps employees from daydreaming on the job or possibly having accidents if they work in a dangerous environment (such as carpentry).

Are not available when their staff need their help.

Plan by arranging a set time every day when you can speak with your supervisor. Many do this first thing in the morning or just after lunch. Another is to leave an e-mail message or place a note on her desk outlining your problem and a time when you *must* have a resolution.

You might ask yourself whether you should be making more decision on your own. Talk to your supervisor and establish your decision-making limits. Prepare sample questions you want to ask including how you think you should handle the problem. You might find that you had the answers all along and just needed your supervisor's approval to use your own initiative to deal with such issues. Your supervisor might be pleased with this sign of initiative or will make herself more available if she doesn't want to delegate extra authority to you.

Won't listen to their staff's suggestions about better ways to complete tasks.

Start by writing down the existing way of doing things. Then add the advantages and disadvantages of doing it the existing way. Do the same with your new way of doing things. Try to concentrate on the cost savings of your plan -

in time and money. Because most companies are money-driven - they'll likely listen if you can prove that your way will save the company money.

Have a negative *"That will never work"* attitude toward changes suggested by their staff.

Are perfectionists and expect everything to be done perfectly.

Talk to your boss. Ask him whether he would rather have things absolutely correct and have you get behind in your work, or continue meeting your deadlines but have a few minor mistakes. You may be surprised at his answer - he may not have realised what kind of pressure you're under and the deadlines you're forced to meet.

S/he may be a perfectionist in everything s/he does and could be a compulsion that s/he can't or doesn't want to change. If this is the case you'll have adapt, by improving your diligence by double checking your work before submitting it to him/her.

Are workaholics and expect their staff to be the same.

At an employment interview, it's important that all prospective employees ask what hours they're expected to work and whether there is much overtime. Many companies state they want their employees to have a work/life balance, but in practice, their staff find it impossible to get their work done in the established business hours. Many are putting in sixty-hour weeks and find themselves taking work home each evening and on the weekends.

Start by discussing your dilemma with your supervisor. Outline your obligations away from work and ask her what she expects of you at work. She may not know that you're juggling things so much and give you pointers on what is and is not crucial to be done at work. You may have to put off your evening courses, if the company can't be flexible.

They're supervising former peers and don't know how to handle the problems that occur.

Those who find themselves supervising former peers are faced with many negative feelings from their former colleagues such as:

jealousy/envy/anger.

they know your weaknesses.

lack respect.

sabotage your efforts.

gang up on you.

expect favouritism or bias; and

are prone to back-stabbing.

If you're younger than your staff, they may not give you the respect you need to get tasks completed. Or if you're a woman supervising men, your subordinates may balk at accepting a female boss (even females staff members may do this). Your supervisor could have eliminated many of these problems by doing his or her part in easing you into your job. S/he should have already talked to each unsuccessful candidate to explain why s/he wasn't chosen for the position. Then on your first day as supervisor, your manager would set up a meeting with your new staff to introduce you. S/he would explain to your new staff that they were expected to give you the same respect and productivity as they did to their former supervisor. S/he would then turn the meeting over to you and leave the room.

How would you start your first meeting where you were supervising former peers? Start on the right foot by acting like a supervisor. After your opening statement, add these comments, *"I'm really counting on all of you to help me make this adjustment."* Then looking each staff member in the eye ask, *"How about you Bill -can I count on your support?"*

Do this for each person in the room. Inevitably there will be one (or even two) who make it obvious by their body language that they're agreeing under duress. You will need to take further steps to deal with these staff members.

Also, state, *"Although I've worked beside all of you since_____, I know little about your individual skills and abilities. In the next two weeks, I'll be looking over your personnel files and will have a discussion with each of you to learn your career plans and know more about your skills and abilities."*

During your meetings with the dissenters, spend time trying to smooth the waters for them. If their productivity drops, take steps to correct their behaviour.

I know you can't go back to your first day on the job as a supervisor, but you could implement these ideas so you can become the supervisor they need.

Upper management have not given supervisors full responsibility to perform their duties (i.e.: Delegate and check staff's work, complete performance appraisals on employees reporting to them.)

Most companies work under the hierarchal system where each level is responsible downward for the next level. No one is expected to infringe on the *"turf"* of the other, unless serious problems surface.

In the following organisational chart, the two supervisors are responsible for two staff each. The manager is responsible for Supervisor 1 and 2. Supervisor 1 is responsible for staff 1 and 2. Supervisor 2 is responsible for staff 3 and 4.

The manager should Not be delegating tasks to any of the staff members. Neither should Supervisor 1 be delegating tasks to staff 3 and 4 or Supervisor 2 to staff 1 and 2.

MANAGER ↓

Supervisor 1 ↓

Staff #1 Staff #2

Supervisor 2↓

Staff #3 Staff #4

To solve these problems, talk to your manager stating, *"I have several problems, and I need your help in solving them. Yesterday Staff member #1 was stretched to the limit to meet some deadlines. I learned that you had delegated another task to him, and he didn't know how to fit it in. On the other hand, Staff member #2 did have time to do your task. In the future could you give the task to me, and I will delegate it downward to the appropriate staff member?"*

Then add, *"When my staff come to you with problems concerning me, would you please ask them whether they have discussed the problem with me? If they haven't, could you please send them to me for a resolution to their problems?"*

"Because it is one of my responsibilities as a supervisor, I'd like to confirm with you the dates I will be conducting the Performance Appraisals for my staff."

Use authoritarian management style, which just results in resistance from staff – Abuse of Power.

This person is only happy when the *"pecking order" is* established. Domineering tyrants must be king of the mountain and anything that gets in his way - he'll crush. He'll use others to get where he wants to go via intimidation. Everything relates to power and many of these people climb the corporate ladder *because* of their ruthlessness. Are they liked? Not by many - but their companies love them because they force their employees to constantly be on their toes. The hair on the back of his staff's neck will automatically rise when he's nearby and their senses will instantly be on high alert preparing them for his next intimidating move.

Speaking to these tyrants about their behaviour will not change their attitude - they don't care what you think. So, the only alternative is to do some sleuthing to find out how many people have left the company because of this tyrant and the approximate cost so far in productivity, unhappy employees, absenteeism because of stress of his staff etc. and approach upper management with the facts. And even when the facts are given, some companies may not act to remove the person.

Supervisor ignores the issue when staff member's behaviour requires correction, the (hoping it will go away) or bungles the disciplinary interview that results in retaliation - rather than a needed change in the employee's behaviour. Again – see Chapter 11 and 10 as well.

To be effective, discipline should be aimed at changing undesirable behaviour - not at initiating retaliation. This supervisor on one hand did nothing about the late employee and over-reacted about a mistake you made. She obviously had not received training on how to discipline staff.

Don't step in to resolve personality conflicts between staff.

This is another sign of poor supervision and especially for the lack of discipline given to the two staff members who are making life difficult and affecting the morale of everyone nearby. The supervisor should call them both into her office and explain her displeasure at their actions.

She would outline the behaviour she objected to by stating, *"This hostility between the two of you can't go on. It's affecting your co-workers and your work. The atmosphere is intolerable, and serious. I know you don't like each other, and I don't expect you to do so, but unless things change and this problem is solved, I'll have to start disciplinary procedures. I'm going to leave you two alone and want you to spend the next ten minutes discussing what you're both going to do to solve this problem. When I return, I want you to tell me what you've decided to do to solve this problem."*

She would then leave the room and return ten minutes later. *"What have you decided?"* By this time, they should have resolved their differences. They would discuss the employee's plans to alleviate the problem, and the supervisor would then ask them, *"Can I count on you to do what you say you're going to do?"* Once they give their assurances the supervisor would add, *"I want you to know that if you revert to your old destructive behaviour, I'll have no other choice but to put written warnings on your file. Do you both understand this?"*

The supervisor will have to keep a close watch on the situation and arrange to have further interviews if warranted.

If they hadn't resolved the problem by the time the supervisor returned, she would take on the role of mediator so that the underlying problems were discussed. If they refused to discuss their differences, then she'd reiterate the earlier comment, *"Unless things change and your behaviour improves, I'll have no other choice but to start disciplinary action. I'm counting on you to not make this necessary."*

If the behaviour doesn't improve - she must follow through with the appropriate action. *The employees must know that the supervisor will not tolerate the situation remaining as it is.*

Show favouritism towards *"pet employees"* (socialise with only one or two of their staff) or show bias (either gender or race related) towards staff members.

Supervisors are human and have their favourites and biases - however in the workplace, this is unconscionable. All employees must be treated equally. If this is your supervisor, have others noticed this behaviour? Are they willing to speak up on your behalf? If so, you could use them to be a witness to the behaviour to back up your allegations. Once this is established, ask for a meeting with your supervisor. Take your witness with you.

State to your supervisor, *"I know that you're probably not aware of it, but you are showing bias against me and favouritism towards Charlie. Here are some facts to back up my allegations."* Hopefully you won't have to take this to your employee relations or Human Resources department but be ready to do so. If your allegations are warranted, you are protected from discrimination by law.

Poor role models. Many of these bad role models are also bullies.

Don't know how to manage their time and become a bottleneck to productivity of their employees. Staff either don't have enough to do or are kept in a panic to complete last-minute assignments. Are wishy washy - can't say *"No"* to requests, so overload staff with assignments.

A boss who isn't organised is often one who has chaos in his or her department. Why not ask your boss if you could help her manage her time better? Suggest that she start a *"to do"* list in the morning that identifies all the tasks he needs to finish by the end of the day. He would then prioritise each of these tasks into A, B, C and D tasks.

"A" tasks must be done right away, by either her or by her staff.

"B" tasks are tackled after "A" tasks are completed.

"C" tasks are done whenever she can fit them in; and

"D" tasks usually should be ignored or thrown away.

When delegating tasks to her staff she could label each request with a coloured tag. Red means that it must be done right away (giving a deadline for completion). Orange means it must be done today, and green - to be done when staff has time. This way, her staff don't have to go through their entire in-basket to determine the priority of tasks. This approach could be used on emails as well.

Why not suggest an early morning meeting where you can discuss your day's assignments and anything you can do to get some tasks on their way? Explain that she's hoarding tasks on her desk to dump on you later when you are rushed.

Allow nepotism with all its unique problems.

This is one of problems that can bring on the downfall of a company. Employees should be hired because of their abilities - not who they know or who they're related to. It's hard fighting this kind of battle and it's too bad you didn't know what you were stepping into when you accepted your position. Unless you want to spend your time alone and fighting the majority - it's far more reasonable and practical to look for work elsewhere.

Don't keep promises.

Supervisors should not make promises unless they intend to keep them. In the future, try to get these promises in writing (CYA - cover your ass) and follow-through later if promises aren't kept. Keep asking your supervisor when your new way will be implemented and describe the hardship cancelling your annual leave is having on your family. When the supervisor makes promises in the future say, *"Can I count on you to do this, because I'll be very disappointed if you renege on your promise?"*

Too immature for a supervisory role - use poor judgement when making decisions.

Some who are in their early twenties make wonderful supervisors, while others in their forties or fifties still don't have enough maturity to supervise staff. It sounds as if she hasn't had supervisory training and seems to be unsure about how she should be doing her job. You won't likely have to do anything about the situation - she will tighten the noose on herself without any help from you. Upper management will soon see that she's not the person for the position.

Why don't you prepare yourself for her downfall by getting the supervisory training yourself, so you're ready to step in when she leaves? Or why not suggest to her that you both take the training (therefore you won't set yourself up to feel guilty later if she fails).

Bring personal problems into the workplace.

This seems to be more of a problem with women who share things with their staff. You'll notice that people at the top of the organization (whether they are male or female) seldom talk about their personal life. They keep the two areas of their lives compartmentalised and all supervisors would be advised to do as well.

Promoted too soon - did not receive proper training to fulfil the obligations of a supervisory/management position.

It's a sad fact that only five to ten percent of all supervisors, foreman, managers, department heads, superintendents, and even CEOs of companies have had adequate supervisory training. Many of these may have MBA degrees and think they have been prepared to supervise others. Unfortunately, most BA and MBA programs do not include that important ingredient. Most supervisors simply clone the behaviours of more senior managers in the company, and unfortunately most of those haven't a clue how to manage people either. It's a never-ending cycle of bad management of a company's most valuable resource – their people.

If any of the above bad supervisory behaviours describe the actions of your supervisors or managers (or you are using them) - seriously consider asking them to change by providing them with the necessary tools they need to do their jobs properly. Will this take a long time and cost too much? No - learning the basics of supervision won't involve as much time as you might expect, and look at the rewards - an effective, productive environment and highly motivated staff!

CHAPTER SEVEN
MAKE TRAINING WORK

You tried to teach an employee a new skill but find that nothing in their behaviour or productivity has changed. Obviously, the training was ineffective.

Learning a new skill:

Teaching someone a new skill takes talent and perseverance. Use of paraphrasing helps implant information. As learners, we all pass through four definite stages when learning something new. These stages are:

Unconscious Incompetence - They aren't even aware that they lack the skill. For example - they may not even have known that the skill of Paraphrasing existed.

Conscious Incompetence - They're aware that they lack the skill. For example, before they learned how to drive a car, they knew they couldn't drive a car.

Conscious Competence - They know the techniques of the skill but had to stop and think before they reacted. *"Do I push the clutch in first or do I turn on the key first?"*

Unconscious Competence - The skill is now well established and automatic. They probably don't even think about what they're doing when they drive - they're on *"automatic pilot."*

It takes six weeks to *"lock into"* how to do something new and up to three months to *"lock-into"* doing something differently than the way they used to.

Retention of information:

Those who're responsible for training have probably thrown their hands in the air at times. Their information seems to go in one ear and out the other with some learners. Many people require constant repetition of instructions. This type of person is probably a poor listener.

Information has a better chance of being *"locked in"* when trainers use a variety of training methods. This could be with visual aids such as movies, PowerPoint presentations or flip charts. To further *"lock in"* the training, see that they use the training as soon as possible.

Training of others:

If you've had the responsibility of training others, you've probably had to explain how to do something more than once. Paraphrasing is a very effective tool to use when training others, especially if they're lazy listeners. To help them retain their training, do the following:

1. Give them short, sequential instructions.

2. State, *"To make sure that I was clear in my instructions to you, could you please explain what you're going to do?"*

3. If they give you a blank look and are unable to relate the steps.

4. Repeat the short, sequential instructions.

5. Again, ask them to relate the steps they will take to complete the task.

You'll find that their listening skills will improve immeasurably. They'll know that when you train them to do anything new, there'll be a *test* to see if they've listened properly. You'll find that instruction-giving will be much easier for you in the future.

Do; however, remember that the onus is on you to make your instructions clear. Using such questions as:

"Do you understand?" (This doesn't confirm that they did understand what you asked them to do).

"Explain what I want you to do." (This will just get their backs up).

"Did you catch that?" (This is a put-down, because you're insinuating that they aren't bright enough to pick up the information).

If they misunderstand you, it's much better to make the problem yours. You can accomplish this by statements such as:

"So that I'm sure I was clear in my instructions to you..."
"Let's see if I've been clear in my instructions to you."

Then ask if they have any questions to clarify the training.

Training vs. development:

Training Need: Exists any time employees require updating of existing skills or need to learn new ones.

Developmental Need: Deals with the full utilisation of the skills of every employee. It uses the abilities learned during training or uses the innate skills of each employee. It's excellent for motivating employees to do their very best and can assist them to reach the *"self-actualisation"* level in motivation.

Development:

When you think of the development of people, what do you usually think of? Formal training, probably. If employees require development, we think of sending them off somewhere else to attend classes, courses, conferences, workshops and seminars. 87 per cent of a person's development takes place on the job and the person's boss is the most important teacher in his/her work life.

Compare development to an elastic band. It expands the knowledge learned in training. Unless a person expands his/her horizons, s/he won't be able to stretch when necessary. Developmental opportunities come up during a normal day, but we often don't think of them as developmental. Let's see if you can identify development vs. training. Assume that your boss said the following things to you. Which statements do you see as Developmental (D) and which as Training (T):

1. What would you recommend?

2. I'm going to show you how our new computer system works. You'll be using it from now on.

3. Tell me only what you feel I should know about your operations and why you feel I should be aware of these things.

4. I'm not going to make your decisions for you, but I'll certainly discuss your problem with you whenever you wish.

5. I'd like you to attend the meeting on safety that all the employees are attending.

6. Please attend this planning meeting in my place. You know our goals and have full authority to commit us to whatever course of action you feel is appropriate.

7. You didn't make the decision to cancel the project soon enough. Let's review it together, to see what we should have done to reduce our losses.

8. Here's a special project for you that will give you experience in a new area. When you finish a plan for accomplishing it, bring it in and show me what you suggest.

9. The head of our treasury group mentioned the fine co-operation he has been getting from you. Keep up the good work.

10. Here's a book on management that I just read. When you've had a chance to read it, let's get together and discuss it. We may find ways of improving our operations.

Only numbers 2 and 5 involved training - the rest are developmental. How did you do?

Career development:

On-the-job career development occurs under these conditions:

Job rotation.
Special tasks.
Acting capacity for more senior position.
Asked for advice.
Team effort.

Allowed to make decisions.
Problem solving.
New duties; or
Assist supervisor in tasks.

Training procedure:

Follow this procedure to set up a training plan to meet training needs:

1. **List problems.** Most training requirements surface when problems occur. Examine these problems to see if they are the real problems.

2. **Determine training needs** to delete problems.

   Here are some Sample Training Needs:

   a. Problem solving capability of several employees requires improvement.

   b. Employees must learn how to handle change or new situations. Communication skills require improvement.

   c. Work ethic and attitude towards work needs to change.

   d. Establish orientation program to help employees understand the organisation better.

   e. Employees must learn how to use our new computer.

   f. Supervisors need to learn how to delegate and motivate their subordinates better.

   g. Time management problems due to overdue reports and work overloads.

   h. A third shift is being put into place. We will need to train another crew to use our equipment.

Set training objectives to meet training need.

These objectives must be realistic and within the scope of learning of the group or person being trained. The objectives must be specific (tangible - easy to measure) rather than general (intangible - difficult to measure). For instance:

General Objective: Improve interpersonal skills of employee

Specific Objective: List 8 steps in the communication process.

Objectives require several pieces of information to be valid (quality, quantity and time). When setting objectives, ask yourself - what is it I want the learner to be able to do after training? After setting the objectives, determine the conditions under which you expect the result to occur: Such as:

a. Given a list of...

b. Without the aid of notes...

c. On the job... Or

d. Whatever help you provide or deny the participant such as: after five hours of dual flight time, the student will be able to land the airplane safely without help from the instructor.

Conditions: After 5 hours of dual flight time, following all safety and flight rules and without help from the instructor, participant will be able to ...

Minimal level of achievement: Will be able to land the airplane safety without help from the instructor.

Write training program. Consider the following when writing a training program:

a. Participants: Size of group, familiarity with subject and their sex (females participate in class participation portions more than men) age, ethnic makeup, belief systems, voluntary/mandatory attendance.

b. Fun: Be creative, exciting, vs. all assignments and work.

c. Time: Task time, reflection time, breaks.

d. Appropriate sequencing.

1. Introduction - get their attention, introduce yourself (if time and appropriate, have them introduce themselves). Explain format and obtain interest/excitement.

2. Body - Present concepts, skills, awareness.

3. Conclusion - What they've learned, what they can use tomorrow, what they can use later, how to retain the information, etc.

   a. **Skill Complexity**: Easy, Difficult, In-between?

   b. **Risk factor** to participants: Light? Heavy?

   c. **Practice**: Instructor demonstration? Class participation?

   d. **Atmosphere** conducive to learning: Comfortable surroundings, attitude of instructor etc.

   e. **Variety**: Lecture, PowerPoint, overheads. media used, length of segments, activity.

   f. **Method of Instruction**: (covered later)

   g. **Intensity of Training**: High? Low?

   h. **Costs:**

4. Evaluate and validate training.

Evaluation: Relates to the methods used in learning during the training. Determine this with the use of tests and follow-up to see if trainees have learned what was taught. This can be done at the end of training or as late as a year later. This is done in class or on-the-job and will use several measuring devices, (how it affected the people involved etc.)

Validation of Training: Relates to the course content of the training session. Was it geared towards reaching the learning objectives? If not - the training wasn't valid and was a waste of training time and effort.

Tangible/intangible behaviour:

When identifying objectives of training, use only tangible behaviours:

Tangible: Measurable and objective such as:

At the end of training, participants will be able to:

Write; recite; identify; differentiate; find; solve; construct; list; show; conduct; demonstrate; choose; express; state;

explain; give; define; relate; determine; describe; present; evaluate.

Intangible: Hard to measure and subjective such as:

At the end of the training, participants will be able to:

Understand; remember; recognise; be aware of; perceive; appreciate; have knowledge of; know; comprehend; be familiar with; realise; be acquainted with.

You will see that the intangible ones would be difficult to measure. Use only tangible and measurable words when setting objectives.

Setting objectives:

To put the training picture in perspective, you will determine the following:

a. Tangible behaviour: Using action words, which describe something you can observe them, doing.
b. Conditions: Explains your method of training and when you expect training to be effective.
c. Minimal Level of Achievement: Usually quantity, quality and time

Here are sample objectives from my ***Train the Trainer*** seminar:

Objectives of Learning:

General: Participants will learn how to prepare and present training programs to meet specific training needs of adult learners.

Specific: (Conditions and minimal level of achievement)

At the end of the seminar, by examining presented information, through discussion, group activities, self-study, assignments, training films and practice lecture, participants should be able to:

(Tangible Behaviour)

Describe 19 qualities of a good training facilitator.

Relate 14 characteristics of adult learners.

Identify learner's needs through 13 training assessment methods.

Explain the meaning of the terms Training and Development and give an example of each.

Write 5 ingredients for setting training objectives.

Define tangible and intangible behaviour and give an example of each.

Show 13 methods of instruction.

Express the meaning of Theoretical and Practical training and where each is used.

Give the differences between Technical and Personal Growth training and give an example of each.

State the uses of 5 different training aids.

Recite 5 steps in the Training Procedure.

Demonstrate 2 kinds of training re-enforcement and give an example of each.

List 6 steps used in one-on-one training that are most effective for retention of information.

Differentiate the 8 steps in the communication process.

Define Paraphrasing and give one example of how it can be used in training.

Relate normal speaking and listening speeds.

Choose 2 methods of keeping participants motivated to learn.

Present 2 tips relating to what instructors should wear when training.

Identifying costs of training:

You'll need to establish training costs to establish a budget. These expenses could be:

1. Room rental.

2. Handouts and overheads.

3. Refreshments and meals.

4. Man-hours of employees who are away from productive work.

5. Equipment rental – PowerPoint projector; video recorder and monitor; overhead projector and screen; slide projector; flip chart, blackboard or whiteboard; podium or microphone.

6. Cost of instructor/resource people - their fee, travelling expenses etc.

7. Notepaper, pens, pencils, binders, name tags, etc.; and

8. Advertising, brochures, emails, etc. (if necessary).

Methods of Instruction:

There are many ways to train participants:

Multi-Media: Many trainers use this method. It uses role-plays, films, cases, lectures etc. and has the multi-media approach. The general idea is to bombard every sense and *"ram"* the message home to the participant. (This is my favourite).

Seminars/Workshops: You can accomplish a lot by these one- or two-day sessions. This rapid orientation is especially effective with an audience that's alert, interested and anxious to learn.

Simulation: Includes such techniques as role-playing, business and other games (computerised or manual). It has the same advantages mentioned for case discussions.

Theory/Practical/Example/Lecture: This is where a trainer explains a complicated theory and gives a practical application of the theory. The trainer then asks participants to give an example of how they could use the theory.

Lecture method: On the surface, it's one of the most efficient methods for imparting ideas. A lecturer in one hour can cover many ideas and/or areas of instruction. Speed of coverage and efficiency is the advantage of the lecture method. Its disadvantage is that much of the lecturer's input can be lost because nothing in the participant's own experience can relate to the information. It's best used in combination with other methods.

Case Studies: Provides cases for participants to study and discuss has become a standard method. The advantage is strong involvement of participants and their own reactions. A disadvantage is the time consumed in writing a good case and in encouraging free and full participation and discussion.

Programmed Learning: These are *"pre-packaged learning systems"* or *"canned sessions."* The major drawbacks are that they're normally very expensive and become obsolete very quickly. A secondary problem is that the facilitator did not prepare the program and may not have enough knowledge to answer participant questions about the content.

Correspondence and Home Study: This method is inexpensive, convenient and can accomplish much. Its weakness is that it lacks immediate feedback and face-to-face contact. Learners require a high level of self-discipline.

Reading: Many training personnel insist that reading changes nothing. Many participants are as adamant that a good book or a good idea in a book has *"changed their life."* It does give a good basis if used as a pre-requisite to those wanting to attend a seminar or as back-up for future use after a seminar.

Laboratory Training: This learning method helps participants analyse their own experiences and identifies other ways they could have handled situations better. Everyone in the group is encouraged to give their input.

Sensitivity Training: Teaches participants how their behaviour affects others and how they can adapt their present behaviour to be more acceptable to others.

Encounter Training: This is an adaptation of sensitivity training. It focuses on body movement, body touch and *"internal feelings."* Its major emphasis would seem to be on heightened awareness and enjoyment of feelings and emotions. This method may be very threatening to some participants.

Situational Training: This method usually begins with some formal program of training. The participants are in *"family groups"* that work and relate together on the job. Usually, an outside trainer helps them to begin the process. The *"work group leader"* takes on more and more of the training responsibility and uses on-going organisational problems as the learning vehicles. It is a learn-as-you-do process and one of the sought-after benefits is to learn how to handle similar future problems. This is also the case when a supervisor involves his/her staff in brainstorming to come up with the best solutions to problems.

Preparing to present a seminar/workshop:

Before presenting a seminar, do the following:

1. Determine the training needs.

2. Make a list of objectives that will meet the training needs using tangible objectives.

3. Research the topic thoroughly.

4. Choose from your research the material what you wish to use.

5. Put into a semblance of order (a) (b) (c) so ideas flow.

6. Provide comments that will bridge between similar areas of study.

7. Brainstorm to determine the best method of presenting the information to the group (through lecture, handouts, films, discussions etc.)

8. Choose which training aids you'll use. Be sure to preview films and that PowerPoint and overhead projectors, videocassettes, slide projector, etc. are all in working order.

9. Prepare a leader's guide.

10. Prepare handouts and overheads.

11. Work out timing for each segment - keeping in mind coffee and lunch breaks. (Remember the need for participants to move around occasionally).

12. Revise program as necessary.

13. Choose class size and room set-up best suited to the program.

14. Determine risk level for participants (group activities are less risky for participants - don't make risks too high at the beginning of the seminar).

15. Set the date for training (be careful choosing day of the week - mid-week seems to suit most people).

16. Have paper, pencils and folders or binders available for participants (optional).

17. Be at training area at least one-half hour before class starts. Make sure all equipment handouts, films etc. are there and in proper working order.

18. Conduct training session.

19. Evaluate and validate training.

Group vs. individual activities:

The risk factor to individuals increases when they have to speak in a classroom situation. Many participants will resist having to speak up in class to relate their experiences or ideas. Others may try to take over the class because they're too expressive in their comments and may dominate the group.

To bring out the quiet ones (using their nametags to identify them) call them by name and ask them for their opinion on the topic. Have different people be spokespersons in group activities.

To quiet down the loud ones - state, *"The class is making John do too much work. It's time to give him a break and for the rest of you to speak up."* In group participation sessions, encourage each participant to express his or her ideas - not just one person. Encourage different people to lead groups (especially the quiet ones).

A facilitator of a seminar must provide a climate of mutual trust, respect and openness, focusing on the positives in themselves and others. In group activities, participants are encouraged to share their problems and fears. There they can gain from the knowledge and resources of others who have been in similar situations and faced similar problems.

Group activities decrease the personal risk factor for learners. It gives several important advantages over one-to-one or individual experiences. Participants find comfort in knowing others share similar difficulties. It's often heard *"I thought I was the only one with that problem!"*

When you divide participants into groups, have them appoint a spokesperson before discussing the topic. Each subsequent group activity has a new spokesperson. As the spokesperson is speaking for the group (not themselves) even the quieter ones will feel less threatened.

In situations where you're pushing for assertiveness in public speaking, have the spokesperson make his/her presentation at the front of the class. Occasionally provide a microphone to increase learning of this new skill.

Technical vs. life skills:

Technical Training:

Use variety in training to keep the interest of participants at technical training sessions. Technical skills range from how to fix your car to how to run your computer. Technical skill training usually involves more homework and more concentration on the part of the trainee. Many participants anticipate (and rightly so) there will be a test after the training. Therefore, the element of risk on the participant is higher. Examples of technical training given in the workplace are:

Supervisory skills of any kind.

Computer training.

Product knowledge.

Selling techniques.

Problem solving and decision making.

Employee discipline; and

Employment interviewing.

Life Skill Training:

These are sessions that help a person grow in other than technical areas. Participants are likely to be more responsive and less threatened at life skills sessions. Examples of Life Skill training are:

Interpersonal skills.

Stress management.

Time management.

Assertiveness training; and

Non-verbal communication.

Theoretical vs. practical training:

Theoretical:

The analysis of a set of facts in their relation to one another. A plausible or scientifically acceptable general principle offered to explain phenomena.

Practical:

Designed to supplement theoretical training by experience. Actively engaged in some course of action.

I use a mixture of the above methods. For example:

a) I introduce a theory i.e. Maslow's Hierarchy of Needs.

b) I give practical examples of the theory. i.e.: When training participants; it's an asset to know where they fit - what motivates them to learn. Is it a need:

(i) to obtain information to fulfil the obligations of their position which would allow them to put bread on the table (Physiological need) or,

(ii) is their job in jeopardy because, if they don't learn the information, they may lose their job (security need) or,

(iv) will they remain behind their peers if they don't obtain the needed information (social needs) or,

(v) they may not obtain a promotion depending on whether they learn the information (ego needs).

c) Have participants decide how this theory and practical application apply to their own specific situation or needs. They're encouraged to give examples of where and when they would use it.

Bridging:

Try to have one topic flow into another by bridging two topics. For example: If I was talking about the different methods I could use, I might bridge onto the topic of costs. I'd say, *"One thing to consider along with what method you choose is the cost of each method of training."* Then I'd bridge into explaining the importance of proper timing of training programs, etc.

Timing of training segments:

I've found that this is a trial-and-error area. You'll have to anticipate how much time to leave for class participation. This is the most unpredictable area of instructing. If you have a quiet group, you may find your timing is all off. If you have a group who really gets into the discussion or (Heaven forbid) get a *"loudmouth,"* you may find yourself running behind.

The first time I present a training program, I put estimated times in the margin of my leader's guide (in pencil). For instance - I'll write in the margin that a segment will run from 10:45 to 11:00 am. As I go through the first run-through, I write, *"needs more time"* or *"took less time"* which I implement for the next session. Soon I have a good idea of how much time I really need. The more proficient you become at presenting seminars, the better you'll become in this area.

Use of training aids:

Training aids are anything that you use to help your participants learn. For example:

PowerPoint projector and computer.

Audio-visual equipment.

DVDs or USBs.

Overhead projector and transparencies.

Slide projector.

Flip charts, either prepared or blank with felt pens.

Handouts/binders. Decide whether you'll give the handouts one at a time, all at once or in packages.

Blackboard or whiteboard plus chalk and felt pens.

Samples of forms or products.

Gimmicks (to lock-in training); and/or

Guest speakers/resource people.

Re-enforcement of training:

Participants want to know ahead of time what's being taught. Being able to measure personal progress increases the participant's motivation to learn and retain the training. They must use the training to retain it. Giving an employee a new skill, they won't use right away, is a waste of training.

For example: Teaching an employee how to be a good supervisor, when it's known that it may be a year until they're able to use the skills. In some cases, they're taught proper supervisory skills, but go back to an environment where their managers haven't had basic supervisory training. These managers balk at the *"new ideas"* their supervisors give them on how they should be doing things.

Make sure that the manager and supervisor receive the same kind of training if you perceive this training is lacking in the manager. Suggest that the managers *"sit in"* on the training session *"so they can monitor how well the supervisors do when they return to work."* This saves face for the manager and results in their receiving the necessary training.

How to keep participants motivated:

If your program has followed the suggestions I've made, you'll find that participants will stay motivated to learn. Watch your audience to see if you're losing them. Look for signs of restlessness, loss of eye contact, fewer questions, yawning. You can get them back by having them move around, give a stretch break, use a little humour. Try telling them they'll be having a test or give a change of pace.

Instructor's apparel:

Trainers should wear comfortable clothing and shoes suitable to the group being trained. Female trainers should not wear bold prints or stripes that are hard to watch for any length of time. Make sure your shoes are *"worn in."*

Presentation skills:

1. Are you projecting your voice properly? Should you be using a microphone for large groups? If so, what kind - on a podium, portable or clip-on? (Check for squeal or feedback).
2. When speaking in front of groups exaggerate your gestures.
3. If you walk while you speak - don't pace back and forth excessively or turn your back to your audience.
4. Don't talk when showing PowerPoint slides, if participants are taking notes from it.
5. Watch for your nervous habits while presenting - such as clicking a pen; hand in and out of jacket pocket; smoothing or stroking hair etc.

6. Use notes - don't rely on memory. You don't have to use them but have them ready in case you lose your train of thought.

7. Use humour occasionally to keep participants interested.

8. Watch your audience for attention level and understanding of what you're explaining.

9. Don't ramble on - be specific.

10. Make eye contact occasionally with members of your audience (short time only - 3 seconds maximum eye-to-eye contact).

11. Dress one level above your audience.

12. Don't use big words. Use technical terms only when necessary.

13. When writing on flip chart or whiteboard - don't stand in front of it; stand to the side, so they can see what you're writing. Don't have your back to them - stand beside your information.

14. A podium helps keep your notes out of sight. Don't; however, spend all your time behind a podium unless you are delivering a speech using a fixed microphone. Use a mobile clip-on microphone if possible.

15. Keep extra strips of masking tape handy. Use these for a multitude of reasons.

16. Have paper and pencil handy to jot down notes for follow-up, especially after group discussions.

17. Have a wrap-up at the end of the seminar to review content of the seminar. Explain to participants that the training is only effective if it's used. Encourage them to follow-up on any areas identified during the session where they need improvement.

Methods I use:

The method I use most often is the multi-media method, especially for one to three-day seminars where people are in one place all the time. For active people, putting them in this kind of environment is not only uncomfortable, but not conducive to learning. Therefore, I must provide variety and movement of the participants to meet this need.

I use lecture, films, overhead projector, PowerPoint, handouts, role-plays, case studies, group and individual activities and discussion periods.

I ask three questions at the end of the seminar. The participants answer them and pass them in (anonymous information). These three questions are:

1. How well did this seminar meet your needs?

2. How could I improve this seminar for the next group?

3. What is the most significant thing you learned today?

CHAPTER EIGHT
CAREER DECISIONS

Possibly the decision you are trying to make stems around your unhappiness with your present job or career. Or it could be one of your staff who is unhappy with the job or career they chose. People often stay in one career because they feel they can't do any other kind of job. This is not true. Most people have what I call transferrable skills. These are skills that they are already using in one job but could be using those same skills in another entirely different career or job.

Career Changes

One woman, who came to me for career counselling was working as a nursing supervisor, but because she now had a young family, found she couldn't adapt to shift work. She was worried that she wouldn't be able to find work in any other occupation. I helped her determine what her transferrable skills were. These consisted of such things as:

An ability to supervise others.

A knowledge of scheduling (to give patients medication etc).

Highly honed interpersonal skills to deal with all kinds of people from uppity doctors to cranky patients.

The ability to keep meticulously detailed reports.

Able to remain calm in emergencies.

Was physically fit; and

Able to make decisions quickly.

These were talents that could be useful in many occupations. She just had to find out which occupation she wanted to try.

She admitted that one of her passions was ladies' fashions. After examining her transferrable skills, I advised her that if she obtained the necessary retail training, her existing transferrable skills could be used as follows:

An ability to supervise others.

A knowledge of scheduling (only she'd be scheduling buying of stock).

Highly honed interpersonal skills to deal with all kinds of people from upset clients to cranky staff.

The ability to keep meticulously detailed reports (stock records, sales, bookkeeping).

Able to remain calm in emergencies (possible robbery or fire).

Was physically fit (would be on her feet most of the day); and

Able to make decisions quickly (when buying stock, marking-down merchandise).

She'd likely have little trouble obtaining a position in a ladies' fashion shop. She decided to obtain the retail training and eventually worked her way up to the position of regional manager of an international ladies' fashion outlet. Her skills as a nursing supervisor prepared her very well for her new career. She just had to fill in the gaps with relevant training.

One fellow (a mechanical engineer) had been very successful in his field, but he had a nervous breakdown at the age of forty. He had met his goals, but suddenly realised he didn't like what he had become or what he was doing! Unfortunately, his father and brother were mechanical engineers, so he had decided to follow their lead. After counselling, he decided that selling would be ideal for him, but he was worried he'd have to take a drastic salary cut that would seriously affect his family's standard of living.

It turned out that he was so close to his problem; he couldn't see that he would be invaluable to many companies. I had interviewed hundreds of engineers and knew he had a unique talent. Many engineers admit they have trouble communicating their ideas either orally or in writing, but this man's communication skills were exceptional. I suggested he contact several firms that produce and sell technically difficult mechanical products to ask them if they required a salesperson with his background. He did so, and within a week, he had received five job offers.

Like many people who come for career counselling, he had no perspective on his situation, so couldn't see his own talents. In career counselling, the counsellor stands back far enough to see things that the individuals can't see for themselves.

Another client, a forty-year-old woman, consulted me when she was thinking about starting a second career. She wanted to be an accountant, but she thought she was *"over the hill and too old to learn."* I asked her how many years she expected to work until retirement. After doing some calculations, *"Twenty-five years,"* she said. Then I asked her my standard question: *"Do you want to stay in a low-level, boring job until then, or would you rather do what you want to do?"* She agreed that she wanted to change but still had serious reservations.

"It will take me four years of university to get the degree I need." I asked her to consider how many years she would still be working after obtaining her degree. *"Twenty-one years."* was her reply. I asked her if the opportunity to spend twenty-one years of her life doing what she wanted to do, would make the sacrifice worthwhile. Her affirmative answer started her on the road to serious career planning.

At any age, you should be thinking about this - especially if you've been marking time in a job you dislike.

Help yourself to a mid-life career change

One life - one occupation? Not any more! Most people who have been in one kind of job for fifteen or twenty years find themselves getting bored with their job even though they like what they're doing. That's the time to seriously think about making a change. There are several kinds of change that can also encourage a change in a career path:

1. Changes in the environment forces individuals to make career changes when:

   Technology changes the nature of an occupation or eliminates it altogether.

   Variations in economic conditions result in high unemployment and inflation.

   When a source of economic support is lost (for example a change in marital status).

2. Changes within the individual requires that a career change be made when:

   A person becomes ill, the illness is work-related. An example of work-related illness is the development of a serious allergic reaction to certain chemicals that require a hair stylist to change occupations.

   When a person is disabled, on or off the job.

   When a person loses former physical or mental capacity as a normal result of aging. (Athletes for example).

3. Changes in the work-world provide greater opportunities for self-initiated change when:

   New technology, and increased affluence and leisure time have created new types of jobs and occupations.

   More non-traditional occupations opening for both men and women. In addition, labour force participation rates are changing to such an extent that women make up nearly half of all employed workers.

   There is greater flexibility in entering and leaving the work force, and the availability of alternative work styles such as flex time and job-sharing.

   There is less social pressure now to stay in one job for a lifetime.

   Greater mobility allows people to move in pursuit of better employment opportunities – even internationally.

This can cause a split from families, friends and support groups.

There is more opportunity to upgrade qualifications and retraining.

3. Changes within the individual, results in a desire to make a career change when:

A person perceives his/her own capabilities differently.

A change in values such as valuing money more than family time or vice versa affects how work is perceived.

The development of new skills opens new possibilities. For example, most clerical positions are now redundant. Many women have taken advantage of their smaller fingers by becoming electronic engineering technologists who repair and keep computers running.

People are coming to realise that the traditional life pattern of choosing an occupation (a group of similar jobs in society such as a chef or salesperson), training for it, entering it, and working at it until retirement, is inappropriate in a dynamic and rapidly changing society. It's not realistic to expect everyone to choose a line of work that's suitable today and will remain so for a lifetime. People today may be employed in five or six jobs. Many will have two or three occupations.

So *"mid-career redirection"* is becoming more commonplace. The homemaker who starts selling real estate, the bank clerk who becomes a para-legal, the engineer who opens a sporting goods store, and the math teacher who becomes a systems analyst are classic examples. Redirection emphasises a change of occupation and not merely the improvement of existing skills or the upgrading of credentials for the same line of work.

Making mid-life career changes

If you're one of the many people considering a mid-life career change, here are some questions you should ask yourself:

1. Am I dis-satisfied with my occupation, or only my job? Could I find satisfaction in a related job within the same field?

2. Do I feel as though I could use more of my abilities and skills in another occupation?

3. Am I and are those dependent upon me willing to make sacrifices so I can start all over in a new occupation?

4. How can I enter my newly chosen field without retraining or further education?

5. What small preparations could I begin today to help me with my occupational switch?

6. How willing am I to take risks – like risking not being happy in a new occupation?

Your nearest Career Centre can provide you with information or counselling on mid-life career change or other career-related topics.

Obstacles holding you back from making a career change

Which of these obstacles are holding you back from making a career change?

Afraid to take risks

Fear that the option chosen may not turn out well. The element of chance can never be eliminated, but through research prior to deciding, you can substantially reduce it. Risks can be further minimised by building flexibility into your plans.

Fear of Failure

Fear is the most paralysing of all emotions. It can stiffen the muscles and stupefy the mind. Have you ever wondered why some people are unafraid to try things you wouldn't have the courage to try? Why is it that others have no problem switching from a very satisfactory job to a better (yet riskier) one? Why do others get married and have a family or go into business for themselves and yet these situations immobilise you?

Join the crowd. We're all afraid of something, which stems from our lack of trust in our ability to handle new situations. If you find yourself worrying about something, ask, *'What am I avoiding now by using my valuable energy with worry?'* The best antidote to worry is action.

Self-confidence and decisiveness often mark leaders in the world. A willingness to take chances, a solid faith in their ability to cope with just about any problem, are characteristics of winners.

If you're growing and changing, you'll experience fear. You'll feel fear whenever you're in unfamiliar territory - but that's normal. Getting rid of the fear is simply a matter of doing something about it and overriding the feeling of helplessness that may accompany it.

Fear of failure is very often the fear of someone else's disapproval or ridicule. Failure is someone else's opinion of how certain acts should be completed. Their perception of what's the right way to do something may differ widely from yours. Neither is wrong. Should a person not succeed at an endeavour, they have not failed as a person. They've simply not been successful at that event, at that moment.

'Without failure we learn nothing.'

Some shun experiences that might bring failure and avoid anything that doesn't guarantee success. They often turn down excellent opportunities but can't explain why they've done so. Or they explain, *'If I was sure I could swing it, I'd try. But...'* if you have this happen to you, ask yourself, *'Why am I not taking this opportunity?'*

Is fear of failure holding you back? Or is it a lack of money, connections, time or possibly anticipated family problems? Learn to analyse why you're being your own worst enemy. Then, decide from time to time, to bite off more than you're sure you can chew.

Mountaineers have all been in the situation where they get themselves into a position where they can't back down; they can only go up. Take the plunge occasionally where you know you'll have to deliver - or else. Unless you're hopelessly in over your head - you'll deliver. You can't acquire the trait of extending yourself to the utmost overnight. Confidence is a cumulative feeling. There will likely be setbacks and disappointments, but:

> *'Someone who tries to do something and fails,*
>
> *is a lot better off than the person who*
>
> *tries to do nothing and succeeds.'*

Fear of disapproval from others

Disapproval from significant others who may disapprove of a career choice for any number of reasons. They may be more concerned about their own needs than the career planner's needs, or they too may be plagued by any of these other fears. Involve these people in the decision-making process. Discuss your career needs and desires with them, and get their assistance when exploring options and involve them in helping to make the final decision. This is particularly important when other people such as family members will be affected by your decision.

Fear of being *"Locked-in"*

You may have the fear that your decision will be unchangeable. The decisions can be reassessed and changed at any time. Sometimes this may be costly or difficult, but once acquired, career planning skills can help the person choose the best way to make a change when it's necessary.

Dissatisfaction with your present situation and/or worries about the future, is often motivation enough to make a person willing to risk taking a chance of changing. The relief often felt after a definite decision has been made and the self-confidence that can come after a rational decision has been reached, can contribute much to motivate you to see your plan through.

Being successful in your chosen career does take time, energy dedication and effort. Don't go into something unless you really want to make a go of it. There's too much competition out there - people who know where they want to go and how they're going to get there. And never *"put your eggs in one basket."* Always have alternative occupations you could investigate, should the economy or technology make your existing occupation redundant.

Think about the successful people you know. Did they put a lot of time, energy, effort and dedication into getting where they wanted to go? You'll probably find they did, because success doesn't come without all those things, and you must be willing to do so as well.

CHAPTER NINE
OTHER PROBLEMS

Another problem people face is not having enough energy to do what they need to do to accomplish everything. They're often full-on at work and get home to a spouse and family responsibilities. It sometimes becomes overwhelming.

Does your energy level depend on what time of the day it is? Are some days of the week better for you than others? If so, try to slot your busy times into those hours and days.

People basically fit into two categories when it comes to use of energy, stamina and how they deal with stressful situations and change. These are Type "A" and "B" personalities:

Detecting Type "A" Personality

Yes No

___ ___ **Vocal explosiveness:** Do you overemphasise key words in ordinary speech and speed up the last few words of a sentence?

___ ___ **Constant motion:** Do you move, walk and eat rapidly?

___ ___ **Impatience:** Do you find yourself hurrying the speech of others or finishing their sentences for them? Is it anguish to wait in line? Do you always rush your reading? Do slow drivers in your lane make you boil?

___ ___ **Thinking or doing two or more things at once:** Do you read a book and watch TV at the same time or read while you eat?

___ ___ **Dominating conversation:** Do you always change the topic to subject that interest you? Is it difficult to restrain from cutting in? When you can't cut in, do you pretend to listen while thinking of something else?

___ ___ **Feeling guilty when relaxing:** Do you begin to lose respect for yourself when you do nothing for a few hours? Do you have few hobbies or diversions outside work? Do you consider non-competitive physical activities a waste of time?

___ ___ **Preoccupation with having – not being:** Do you fail to find time to improve yourself or explore new and interesting things? Have you neglected the aesthetic side of life for the sake of accumulating achievements?

___ ___ **Scheduling more and more in less and less time:** Do you fail to make allowances for unforeseen contingencies? Do you always feel pressured by time? Do you create deadlines if none exist?

___ ___ **Feeling compelled to challenge others:** Do you find yourself competing even when the situation doesn't warrant it?

___ ___ **Nervous tics or gestures:** Do you frequently clench your fist, bang your hand on the table, or pound your fist into your palm to drive home a point? Do you habitually clench your jaw or grind your teeth?

___ ___ **Fear of slowing down:** Do you feel that your success is due to your ability to do things faster than others?

___ ___ **Attachment to the numbers game:** Do you find yourself committed to translating achievement in terms of quantity instead of quality?

___ ___ **TOTAL SCORE**

Type "A" people love change, hate routine and can be very high achievers should they channel their behaviour in the right direction. They usually have a very high energy level that at times can become hyperactive. They have a high work ethic and have difficulty relaxing. Most feel that if they relax they're not producing, so usually find something productive to do. They're often seen doing two or three things at once. They make quick decisions and become very annoyed with those that don't have this quality. Some can become manic and burn themselves out – many are workaholics and need to learn to balance their work/home lives.

What to do about Type "A" Personality

Are you spending your time doing what's important to you - career, family and social? Are you doing more and more and accomplishing less and less? If so, the following may help you:

1. Establish career and life goals.

2. Learn time management - set priorities.

3. Know that you shouldn't feel guilty if you're not busy.

4. Spend time on things of importance to you.

5. Take regular coffee and lunch breaks.

6. Spend some time alone - possibly in a nature setting and *"get away from it all."*

Detecting Type "B" Personality

Yes No

____ ____ **Vocal quietness:** Do you speak so softly that others ask you to repeat yourself?

____ ____ **Slow motion:** Do you normally have to keep reminding yourself to *"get going,"* which makes you late for appointments?

____ ____ **Patience:** Do you find that waiting in line never bothers you or you drive below the speed limit? Do you get beeped at by other drivers because you're not keeping up with traffic?

____ ____ **Thinking or doing two or more things at once:** Do you find you're confused if you're attempting to do more than one thing at a time, or you prefer a repetitive job?

___ ___ **Lacking in conversation skills:** Do you find you spend most of your time listening rather than speaking when in a group?

___ ___ **Your own ability to relax:** Do you enjoy loafing around and have difficulty *"getting your act in gear?"*

___ ___ **Scheduling less and less in more and more time:** Do you fail to meet deadlines or run out of energy long before the day is over? Do you seem to accomplish less now than you did before?

___ ___ **Feelings when challenged by others:** Do others intimidate you or you feel threatened by their successes?

___ ___ **Nervous tics or gestures:** Do you display nervous habits when you feel rushed or intimidated?

___ ___ **Fear of slowing down:** Do you believe that it's natural that you should be slowing down - you're older than you were when you were at top speed?

___ ___ **Anxiety:** Do you feel that you have little control over your life? Do you often feel inadequate, uneasy, unfulfilled, not satisfied with where you are, or what you're doing, but haven't taken the challenge of changing?

___ ___ **TOTAL SCORE**

Type "B" people hate change, like routine and are usually low to average achievers. They often need an "A" type person to get them motivated. They usually have a low to average energy level that at times can become lethargic. Some lack a strong work ethic and have few problems relaxing. Most feel that there's far too much they're expected to do, and can find themselves frazzled at the end of the day. They have difficulty doing two or three things at once. They're slow at making decisions and become upset when others insist they make instant decisions. Some can suffer from burnout trying to keep up with other's demands and the pressures they feel are being imposed on them.

What to do about Type "B" Personality

1. Are you in a dead-ended job that's causing you to feel lethargic which encourages a low energy level? If so, change jobs.

2. Are you using your potential - or are you floating through life – existing rather than living?

3. Establish set, written goals and set out to achieve them.

4. Set priorities. Don't waste time on trivial items and don't be a perfectionist.

5. Don't remain a follower - become a leader - participate fully - don't just become another body in a group.

6. Stop procrastinating - do it today! Give yourself rewards for getting things done.

7. Build your self-image - take an assertiveness course.

8. Cultivate friends who encourage you to do your best - become a positive thinker.

Introvert and Extrovert Personality Types

Another problem you could face might stem from your ability to communicate with different types of personalities.

It's important to analyse where people fit in relation to their wants, needs and desires and their ability to deal with issues. Analyse this person - see how you can more effectively deal with their reactions to situations by evaluating where they fit in the following three categories:

Extreme introvert: This is an extremely careful person, is contemplative and analytical, leans toward perfectionism, and can work doggedly at detailed work. Introverts tend to be a 'cerebral' type of person concerned with affairs of the mind rather than a lot of physical activity. *Many may resist change.*

Extreme extrovert: This person is more action-oriented, prefers to get started quickly, deciding on details along the way (or ignoring them altogether, thinking someone else will take care of them). Extroverts may get many things started but leave some details unfinished. *They enjoy change.*

Combination introvert/extrovert: This person combines some attributes of both the introvert and the extrovert and is a balance of the two extremes. Their individual actions would tell you which phase they are in at that time.

Common ways extreme Introverts feel and behave:

Don't like to lend things to others. They'll do it, but with much hesitancy and caution.

Would rather make a report in writing than give it verbally.

Can be very blunt and straightforward.

Are more reserved in their laughter or other displays of feelings and emotion.

Are very careful with their personal possessions. Keep things looking nice and in good order.

Are slow in action and decision-making.

Considered perfectionists by many. Write and rewrite until everything's perfect.

Become embarrassed quite easily.

Are chronic worriers.

Are quite concerned and deliberate about most routine decisions.

Are very sensitive about comments made about them.

Resent autocratic commands from others.

Can be extreme in religion, politics and other social issues.

Tend to struggle alone with problems.

Quite comfortable working alone, rather than as a member of a team.

Enjoy and need praise and recognition but won't ask for it.

Tend to be suspicions.

Are moodier than a strong extrovert.

Enjoy work requiring precision and attention to detail.

Prefer intellectual pursuits.

Daydream a lot and think about what might have been or what is yet to come.

Are extremely conscientious and berate themselves for less than perfect performances.

Common ways extreme Extroverts feel and behave:

Lend money and possessions readily.

Fluent talkers; can give reports better orally than in writing.

Usually, careful not to hurt others' feelings and want to be liked by others.

Laugh readily.

Don't take care of personal possessions.

Make decisions quickly.

Are quick in their actions. Seldom rewrite letters or give attention to detail.

Hard to embarrass.

Aren't worriers.

Aren't bothered by details of what wear, what to eat, where to go, etc.

Aren't very concerned by what's said about them.

Accept orders as a matter of course.

Are usually moderate in their religion, politics and other social issues.

Don't hesitate to ask for help in solving problems.

Would rather work with others than alone.

Make their own opportunities for praise.

Aren't suspicious of others' motives.

Are in about the same mood always.

Prefer work where details are not important.

Prefer athletics to books and *"high brow"* activities.

Are not great planners - take things as they come?

Are risk-takers and gamblers - seldom worry about the consequences?

Sensory Language

It's possible that you might be communicating in an ineffective way with others. For instance you have sent several emails to someone and they haven't replied. With another, you've left many phone calls – but they never reply.

When we say two people have *"rapport,"* we usually mean that their relationship is harmonious - we get into someone else's world. We will not be able to do this unless we adapt to *their* needs. We can enhance this rapport by determining others' primary sensory language. Most of us are a mixture of all three, but one usually stands out as being our primary sensory language.

People process information in different ways. They are primarily *visual, auditory* or *kinaesthetic* (muscular movement) in the way they process information. Each type uses distinctive words that reflect their preference. To create rapport with people, listen to find their primary mode of communication then mirror their language. Here are examples of these:

The visual person might say:

'I get the picture.'
'I see what you mean.'
'Let me see what the job looks like.' Or,
'My perception is...'

The auditory person uses such phrases as:

'That sounds good to me.'
'I hear what you're saying.'
'That rings a bell.'

'I hear you loud and clear.'
'She's not in tune with me.' Or.
'Let me explain how this works.'

Typical phrases for kinaesthetic would be:

'Show me how to do this.'
'That doesn't feel right.'
'Hold on.'
'I'm comfortable with that.'
'I'll give you a feel for the job.'
'I grasp what you're saying.'
'That's a rough problem.' Or,
'You have a heavy task.'

So often a person's use of the above words can give you a clue as to what type of sensory language they want to use. You might be a verbal person and expect to communicate with others that way. However, the other person is a visual person, so is more comfortable using the written word. I, for instance, don't seem to be able to remember people's names unless I see the name printed out – yes, I'm a visual person not an auditory one. I often have problems communicating with one of my friends. When she gives me complicated information; I write it on paper. She asks what I am doing, and I must explain that I won't remember the complex information she is giving me unless I write it down. She doesn't seem to understand this. So, I solved the problem by explaining sensory language to her.

Now, do the following:

Determine your primary sensory language.

Determine the primary sensory language of the people you deal with.

What changes can you make so you can communicate on the wavelength as your difficult people?

How to keep from being misunderstood

Here are a few common sense guidelines to help ensure that you won't be misunderstood:

Start with clear thinking:

Pause to collect your thoughts before you speak. In a one-to-one conversation, don't feel that you have to jump right in with a response the second the other person finishes speaking.

Sort out what you want to say:

This lets the other person know that you're taking time to digest what s/he has said. If you jump right in - it's probably an indication to him/her that you're not listening.

Choose your words carefully:

Don't use big words just to impress your listener. Try to avoid words that have double meanings. Remember that words don't carry the same meaning from one part of the country to the next. You have to put yourself in the other person's place - try to understand his/her point of view and what s/he brings to the conversation to discussion.

Watch for non-verbal signs of agreement or disagreement:

In face-to-face conversation, much of what we communicate is non-verbal, and we need to learn how to read the signals correctly. Sometimes the person will nod absent-mindedly, as if s/he is agreeing with you. However, s/he may not agree with you at all. S/he may even be thinking about something entirely different from the subject you're discussing. Other non-verbal signs - a smile, a frown, a questioning look, a fidgeting listener - give you signals on whether or not you're being understood. Don't overlook these non-verbal signs, but don't put too much emphasis on them either. Watch their eyes. Eye contact is important in communicating effectively.

Be a good listener:

You can't effectively respond to what the other person is saying if you're thinking about where to go out to dinner, or trying to analyse why you had a fight with your spouse that morning. To be a good listener, you have to concentrate - and concentration requires discipline. Clear your mind of other thoughts and problems; give the other person your full attention. Look the speaker in the eye, rather than letting yourself glance around the room at things that may distract you.

Speak clearly and distinctly:

A r t i c u l a t e - don't mumble! More than one misunderstanding has occurred for the simple reason that the listener didn't hear it the same way you thought you said it. This is especially important if you have an accent or if you're speaking with people whose native language is not the same as yours. Try to use well-known English words.

Writing skills:

Most of these same basic guidelines apply to the written word, except that you don't have any way to watch the other person's reaction. Thus, in writing, it's even more critical that you organise your thoughts, choose your words carefully, and present your message in such a way that it can't be misunderstood. The new way of writing letters is to write as if you were talking with the receiver. You won't be able to say, *"But this is what I meant!"* when the other person is reading your letter, email or report.

What could I improve?

Expressing information, ideas, suggestions:

1. Being brief, concise and getting to the point.

   Need to do it less?

   Doing all right?

   Need to do more?

2. Being definite rather than hesitant and apologetic.

   Need to do it less?

   Doing all right?

   Need to do more?

3. Talking in specifics, giving examples, details.

   Need to do it less?

Doing all right?

Need to do more?

4. Talking in generalizations.

Need to do it less?

Doing all right?

Need to do more?

Expressing Feelings:

Letting others know when:

1. I don't understand something they've said.

Need to do it less?

Doing all right?

Need to do more?

2. I like something they've said or done.

Need to do it less?

Doing all right?

Need to do more?

3. I disagree with them.

Need to do it less?

Doing all right?

Need to do more?

4. I'm getting irritated.

Need to do it less?

Doing all right?

Need to do more?

5. I feel hurt or embarrassed.

Need to do it less?

Doing all right?

Need to do more?

Understanding information, ideas and suggestions of others:

1. Listening to understand, rather than to prepare my next remark.

   Need to do it less?

   Doing all right?

   Need to do more?

2. Helping others to participate in the discussion.

   Need to do it less?

   Doing all right?

   Need to do more?

3. Before agreeing or disagreeing, check to make sure I do understand what others mean (using paraphrasing.)

   Need to do it less?

   Doing all right?

   Need to do more?

4. Summarizing points of disagreement.

   Need to do it less?

   Doing all right?

   Need to do more?

5. Asking questions in ways that get more information than *"yes"* or *"no."*

   Need to do it less?

   Doing all right?

   Need to do more?

Understanding and responding to others' feelings:

1. Checking out with others what I think they're feeling, rather than assuming I know.

   Need to do it less?

   Doing all right?

Need to do more?

2. Responding to a person who is angry with me, in such a way that I don't ignore his/her feelings.

Need to do it less?

Doing all right?

Need to do more?

3. Responding to a person whose feelings are hurt in a way that I don't ignore his/her feelings.

Need to do it less?

Doing all right?

Need to do more?

4. Responding to a person who is expressing closeness and affection for me in such a way that I don't ignore his/her feelings.

Need to do it less?

Doing all right?

Need to do more?

5. Surveying a group to determine how much agreement exists (in making a group decision).

Need to do it less?

Doing all right?

Need to do more?

General:

1. Talking in group discussions.

Need to do it less?

Doing all right?

Need to do more?

2. Getting feedback, encouraging others to let me know how my actions affect them.

Need to do it less?

Doing all right?

Need to do more?

3. Being aware when I'm trying to cope with my own feelings of discomfort rather than responding to the other person's feelings.

Need to do it less?

Doing all right?

Need to do more?

4. Accepting help from others.

Need to do it less?

Doing all right?

Need to do more?

5. Offering to help others.

Need to do it less?

Doing all right?

Need to do more?

6. Yielding to others, giving in to others.

Need to do it less?

Doing all right?

Need to do more?

7. Standing up for myself.

Need to do it less?

Doing all right?

Need to do more?

Listening problems

Problems in listening occur when the recipient of the information:

1. Has a closed mind

2. Is too lazy to think.

3. Is distracted by other things.

It takes perseverance, discipline and hard work to overcome the above. Several things will assist you:

a. Maintain eye contact with the person that is speaking as much as is comfortable (maximum - 3 seconds). Don't allow your gaze to wander around the room.

b. Control your mind. Keep from wandering away from the subject. Use your thinking speed positively and effectively. Remember, a person speaks at 125 - 150 wpm and can think 750 - 1,200 wpm. Ask yourself questions about what you already know about the subject being discussed.

c. Don't run off at the mouth - (make your mouth your worst enemy). Be an observer. Listen to everything a person has to say before attempting to answer or make your comments.

d. Keep an open mind.

e. Listen totally - not half way.

f. Don't be prejudicial - keep a clean screen.

g. Don't jump to conclusions.

Samples of closed minds:

Inflexible attitudes - cannot be swayed in their opinions. Black is grey, no matter how many people may argue that it is BLACK. This is the opposite of creativity. You don't have to give up on your ideas, only you don't have to argue with others. Give alternative solutions.

Laziness - TV and radio makes us lazy listeners. We hear only one-quarter to one-half of what's being said. We do, however remember commercials, especially if set to music. Our subconscious mind picks them up even if we aren't consciously listening.

People who jump to conclusions.

Prejudice - age, sex race.

CHAPTER TEN

MEETING PROBLEMS

Some problems involve meetings. Smoothly run meetings are a rarity. For instance, you chair a meeting, delegate assignments to your group, have a follow-up meeting and get these comments:

"I didn't know I was responsible for that?"

"I didn't agree to do that!"

"I thought you didn't need that till next week!"

The most important person at a meeting is the facilitator or chairperson. His/her main functions are to:

Keep things running smoothly;

Keep participants motivated; and

Get things done.

If you are chairing a meeting you should have:

a. Planned your meeting.

b. Prepared for your meeting.

c. Known how to chair a meeting.

d. Understood meeting traps; and

e. Know how to handle problem participants.

Groups don't function properly without a formal or informal leader. One of the measures of your success at chairing a meeting is your ability to lead others.

Conducting meetings:

Supervisors may hold weekly or monthly meetings with their staff (normally held in their own facility). Other times, supervisors may hold informal meetings on-site (at field sites) where the employees complete their tasks. Or they may be called upon to chair a meeting that includes supervisors from other offices, branches or cities. These meetings may be held in a meeting room of a hotel, in the boardroom of another company or in their own facilities.

Therefore, supervisors need to understand how to chair meetings properly so they can attain the desired results.

Overcome cultural or personality differences:

If a personality clash happens at a meeting, stop the members involved. Arrange for a meeting later with the people, so you can discuss the problems identified by the clash. Then bring the group back on track by suggesting, *"Let's get back to the topic we were discussing. I need all of you to concentrate on reaching the objectives of this meeting."*

If the leader is dealing with people of different cultural backgrounds, it's important that s/he understands what makes that person tick. Discourage any discrimination shown towards meeting participants. Jokes at the expense of someone else are not jokes at all. Discourage such discriminatory comments by stating, *"I didn't think that was funny, Paul."*

If Paul states, *"I was only kidding."* reply, *"Paul, your comments were a put-down to Harry. If your comments are as harmless as you say they are, then they're pointless and a waste of time. Keep these kinds of comments to yourself."*

Evaluate:

The leader must constantly assess the feelings of the group, as well as the group's progress toward accomplishing the task. The chairperson may have to table some issues for a later meeting, because crucial information was not available.

Follow-up:

Make sure members are aware of what they're to do and follow up. It's fine to decide that Peter will oversee doing something, but if Peter doesn't do what he says - the meeting won't accomplish all its objectives.

Before the meeting adjourns, ask each person to relate what s/he must do towards reaching your team objectives. Then state, *"Peter, can I count on you to do...?"* After the meeting, send each member a copy of the minutes of the meeting that includes information about delegated tasks.

Preparing for a Meeting:

1. Set specific goals for the meeting. Know what you want to accomplish and when.
2. Determine what decisions must be made at the meeting and those that can wait.
3. Establish time frames for each topic on the agenda.
4. Set up plans of action to deal with #2.
5. Decide who will attend the meeting. Delete any that cannot benefit or give assistance at the meeting. Expect and encourage everyone to participate fully.
6. Prepare an agenda and distribute to those invited to attend the meeting. Contact participants and explain what part they'll play in the meeting (what you want from them). Make sure they're able to attend the meeting or will send a knowledgeable person in their place.
7. Choose a time and place that's most suitable to the attendees. The physical surroundings affect the atmosphere of the meeting. For instance, the temperature of the room, seating and involvement of members. Remember access to the room (wheelchairs?) its size, preferably movable furniture, the acoustics, lighting and whether there are adequate parking and rest room facilities.
8. Arrange to have someone available to take notes and get refreshments. (Don't assume that one of the female members should do this).
9. Anticipate
   a. Costs.
   b. Problems (i.e. crucial members can't come to the meeting).
   c. Objections (legitimate or otherwise).
   d. Arguments (regarding the necessity of your goal. Have facts available to back up your idea).

e. Personality problems that might surface between participants attending the meeting.

10. Prepare handouts and other back-up material essential for the meeting. Have facts, not assumptions to back up your ideas. Use a little showmanship by making your presentations interesting and informative. Use PowerPoint presentations, overheads, flip charts, computer printouts, anything that makes what you're discussing clearer to the participants.

11. Make up name cards for the tables, so people can address others by name. (Not required when attendees know each other).

12. Smoking has become a very touchy subject. Consider the comfort of all participants and decide whether this will be allowed at the meeting, at coffee breaks or not at all. My research proves that this is one of the pet peeves of non-smokers. They resent being forced to attend meetings where they have no choice but to sit in a smoky room. Those with allergies may have traumatic physical reactions. Try to allow smokers adequate *"smoke breaks"* away from the meeting room if allowed in the building.

13. Discourage outside interruptions. Ask participants to turn off their mobile phones and have messages taken for them unless they are emergency situations. Try to have the meeting place away from the normal work setting to discourage this.

Avoiding planning blunders:

1. Meeting planners often plan with no data about the participants, nor their hopes and expectations about the purpose of the meeting.

2. If you're planning a meeting, identify:

Who's coming:

Why they're coming; and

What specifically is to be accomplished at the meeting?

3. Lack of involvement in the planning by those who'll be at the meeting. When you don't involve participants in some direct way, they'll probably not take an active part or may not even come to the meeting. They probably feel they'll be wasting their time attending the meeting.

4. Beautiful, but illegible visual aids. You may find that your visual aids are visually pleasing, but you may find that when you try them out in a large room, you can't see them. Check all your visual aids in the room where they'll be used. Make sure that PowerPoint computer programs, video recorders and overhead projectors are in good working order and extra bulbs are available for projector.

5. Same meeting, same place, same time and objectives. Though sameness gives security to some, it bores others to tears. Why not vary the place and time of the meeting to suit different people in the group?

6. Holding meetings only because they're scheduled to be held. If there's no real reason or agenda for a meeting, why hold it? Can you imagine how motivated members would be if they could count on its being meaty and full of content? They should know that if there's nothing to discuss you'll cancel it.

7. Lack of plans if extra people turn up. Often meetings planned for 50, have 75 or 100 people attend. Can the room be made cosier if the opposite happens and fewer people than were planned arrive? It's important to have some contingency plans.

8. No agenda or the one that omits the purposes for this meeting.

9. Too many items/activities planned for the time available. A realistic plan is needed to determine how much time various items or activities will take. If you have more items than the time allows, then;

Cut out some items.

Increase the meeting time.

Arrange to put them in as pieces.

Work on in small groups during the meeting; or

Have two meetings.

The use of questions at meetings:

1. Overhead Question – are those you direct to everyone in the room - used to stimulate ideas. For instance: *"What can we do to reduce traffic problems in our parking lot?"*

2. Direct Question – are directed to a specific participant.

   For Instance: *"Do you have any ideas, Gerry?"*

3. Relay Question - participant asks a question of leader for opinion or information.

   For Instance: *"What do you think we should do?"*
   The leader relays to the rest of the group:
   "Let's hear from the rest of you." or *"What do you think, Gerry?"*

4. Reverse Question - question asked of the leader where the participant already has an idea of what will work:

   For instance: (Question) *"What do you think we should do about the parking-lot problem?"*

   (Leader) *"I'm not sure. What do you suggest?"*

Here are some questions and how they can be worked into a meeting:

1. Where used: To redirect the discussion

   How used: *"How do you feel about this new idea?"*
   Tips on use: Repeat the question as you redirect it.

2. Where used: To avoid experting.

   How used: *"What do the rest of you think about this?"*
   Tips on use: Repeat the question as you redirect it.

3. Where used: To open discussion.

How used: *"We need to determine the cost of building a new parking lot."*

Tips on use: Plan specific questions that ask for input from participants.

4. Where used: To get agreement and acceptance.

How used: *"Does that express your idea?" "Can you give us an example of what you mean?"*

Tips on use: Ask for specific examples. Use paraphrasing.

5. Where used: To conclude the discussion.

How used: *"Are there any other points to be considered?"*

Tips on use: Then move on to the next topic.

6. Where used: To provoke thinking.

How used: *"What do you think of that idea?" "What are the advantages?" "What are the dangers?"*

Tips on use: Pause to allow time for thought.

7. Where used: To secure participation.

How used: *"Bill, what's your experience with this?"*

Tips on use: Have questions in reserve.

8. Where used: To guide discussion or bring it back on track.

How used: *"How does that relate to our topic? What point are we considering?"*

Tips on use: Build questions on previous responses.

Role of the chairperson:

The chairperson's role in any group situation is to help achieve the objectives defined for the meeting. Other functions include:

Planning a meeting:

Planning for a meeting usually is done in the form of an agenda that may or may not have input from meeting members. The planning will include deciding where and when to hold the meeting, what will be discussed and by whom and ordering the necessary audio-visual equipment. A copy of this agenda will be sent to all participants so they can bring the necessary documents and information to the meeting.

During the meeting, the leader should consider how to deal with such situations as:

1. Is the group moving towards meeting the objectives?

2. Are individual needs being met, as well as group needs?

3. Is the meeting climate psychologically conducive for changes to take place?

4. Are participants working harmoniously with each other?

5. Use and develop group's unique talents and abilities:

If members of the meeting are your subordinates, check their personnel files to determine their areas of expertise. One may be an exceptional organiser so you'd delegate things that would bring out this talent. However, if you aren't aware of this skill, you may delegate the responsibility to a less qualified member.

If you don't have access to personnel files (possibly person works for another department or company) ask them to volunteer for things they can handle.

At meetings, try to provide an atmosphere that shows people they're important. Don't interrupt - listen to what they have to say. Occasionally, you'll have to reject ideas. When rejecting ideas, you need to explain why. Make sure members know you're rejecting their idea, not them. Do this by encouraging further input and ideas from them. Never label people in any way i.e. *"How dumb can you be! We've tried that twice before and it didn't work."*

Encourage an atmosphere conducive to change. Show them you encourage new ideas and ways of doing things. Bring out their creativity.

Use *"brainstorming sessions"* when tackling problems. Encourage a free-wheeling atmosphere that encourages new, innovative ideas. This process enables you to have Plan B and C on the back burner if Plan A doesn't work.

If participants stray off topic, bring them back with such statements as *"We're getting off track. We were discussing... Does anyone have an idea?"*

How to chair a meeting:

Send a copy of your agenda to each person attending the session. Include information relating to what document-tation, files or input you expect from each participant. Then proceed as follows:

1. Open the meeting:

    a. Put the group at ease with a cordial greeting.

    b. Have participants identify themselves - where they're from, who they work for, etc. – establish their credibility so their suggestions and input are heard (not necessary if participants know each other).

    c. State the purpose of the meeting - what objectives are expected.

    d. Identify the problems or ideas for discussion using common words so everyone at the meeting can understand your idea or problem. (A public speaking course might help in this area).

    e. Outline the content of the meeting.

       For instance: *"First we'll... Then we'll... There will be a coffee break at..."*

2. Present first problem or idea:

    a. State the facts.

    b. Ask questions, to overall group or directly to an individual or to more knowledgeable participants.

3. Conduct the discussion:

    a. Encourage participation from *all* participants. If some aren't actively participating, ask them a direct question they can't answer with a *"yes"* or a *"no."*

b. Control the discussion - avoid personal feelings that could result in arguments.

c. Prevent anyone from monopolising the discussion.

d. Keep the discussion on track.

e. Analyse the progress of the discussion.

f. Use paraphrasing to confirm opinions expressed by others.

4. Summarise discussion:

a. Identify the highlights of the meeting.

b. Evaluate ideas, opinions and experiences.

c. Arrive at conclusions or solutions - what the meeting accomplished.

d. Decide on a plan of action - how to handle the problem or idea using group recommendations and/or decisions when applicable.

5. Present next problem or idea:

Follow above procedure until you have discussed all the items. Don't go on to another topic until the group has decided or follow-up meeting arranged for each item.

Note: Watch participant's (and your) body language. You'll be able to tell whether you're coming on too strongly, too softly and if your presentation is too boring to keep their attention. Make direct eye contact with as many people as you can so they feel included in the proceedings.

Stand up if you feel the need to appear more forceful. If you wish a more informal atmosphere, sit down. Listen to ideas. Be willing to change your mind.

Types of meetings:

You have a meeting but find that things don't happen the way you want them to. What kinds of problems are you likely to face and how can you deal with them and accomplish your aims?

There are two basic kinds of meetings:

Information meetings: To pass on information which the participants don't have.

1. State the purpose of the meeting and the major topic of discussion.

2. Provide information in as much detail as necessary for full understanding. Carefully explain background information.

3. Allow questions and feedback so the chairperson knows:
   a. Whether the participants understood the information; and
   b. How they accept it. Participants have the opportunity of clarifying anything that's not clear to them.
   c. Summarise the major points covered and any issues that require clarification.

Discussion meetings: These are used:

   a. To solve a problem or develop a plan of action.

   b. To obtain ideas or suggestions which can be used later to make the decision or

   c. To make the best use of the ability and experience of personnel.

Follow these steps:

1. State the problem or idea.

2. Identify the extent of the participants' involvement to:

   a. Solve the problem.

   b. Make suggestions.

   c. Formulate a plan upon which management can decide.

3. Generate ideas, discuss, evaluate and formulate a plan or reach a decision that represents the consensus of the participants.

4. Summarise meeting to:

   a. Make certain everyone understands and agrees with decision

b. Make sure everyone knows what they're to do following the meeting, if you require such action. (Very important).

Meeting traps:

1. The un-briefed resource person or speaker.

This person comes in and has no idea what you really wanted or what the group is like and gives the usual canned speech that's *always* given on that topic by that person.

2. Agenda not shared

There's only one copy of the agenda available and the chairperson has it. It's hard for participants/members to feel involved when they can't see and understand plans of the meeting.

3. Formal, classroom-style seating

This is rows of chairs all facing the front. This gives the participants the non-verbal clue that all action and wisdom, comes from the front of the room. It makes it difficult or impossible for them to participate actively.

4. Meeting starts with nothing to do for early arrivals

If you know that your meeting will have a raggedy start, plan something for the *"early birds"* to do, discuss or think about.

5. Long introductions of speakers, consultants, helpers

This usually produces psychological distance between them and the participants. Give a short, warm welcome instead of a long prologue. Often speakers have ideas on how they would like you to introduce them. Some will want to introduce themselves.

6. Long, drawn-out, windy speakers

Often people go longer than the limits they're given. It's important to go over the ground rules with them at the beginning of the meeting. You might introduce the speaker and say, *"The time of the following presentation is 12 minutes."*

7. **Total reliance on the one expert at the meeting**, rather than using that person to help uncork the resources of all the participants.

8. **Coffee breaks too long or short**

If too long, they may disrupt the continuity. Consider having water, coffee, tea and juice available throughout the meeting with just a short bathroom break if the meeting goes over two and a half hours. You may decide that coffee break is too short, which may not give participants the opportunity of getting to know fellow meeting participants.

9. **Failure to deal with feelings of participants**

Often groups are so task-oriented that they skip even everyday manners and may appear abrupt. For example: some people have excellent ideas, but shyness holds them back from offering them because of the atmosphere. Leader must ask direct questions to this person to obtain their active participation.

10. **No record of what happened at a meeting**

It's important that someone takes notes and documents meetings. These then become a history of those meetings, which defines plans, as well as decisions and commitments made by participants. Copies of these minutes are given to each person who attended the meeting.

11. **Follow-up**

Neglecting to carry the group *"into the future"* to guarantee that the work of the meeting will pay off. i.e.: Be sure to decide who will do what and when and obtain commitments from them that they will do what they said they would do.

Dealing with problem participants at meetings

Participant is: Overly talkative - to the extent that other participants do not have an opportunity to contribute.

Participant may be: An 'eager beaver,' exceptionally well informed; naturally wordy or nervous.

What to do: Interrupt *with 'That's an interesting point... Let's see what everyone else thinks.'* Directly call on others. Suggest *'Let's put others to work.'* When the person stops for a breath, thank him or her, restate the pertinent points and move on.

Participant is: Engaging in side conversations with others in the group.

Participant may be: Talking about something related to the discussion; discussing a personal matter or uninterested in the topic under discussion.

What to do: Direct a question to the person. Restate the last idea or suggestion expressed by the group and ask for the person's opinion.

Participant is: Argumentative – to the extent that others' ideas or opinions are rejected, or others are treated unfairly.

Participant may be: Seriously upset about the issue under discussion; upset by personal or job problems; intolerant of others; lacking in empathy or a negative thinker.

What to do: Keep your temper in check. Try to find some merit in what's said, get the group to see it too; then move on to something else. Talk to the person privately and point out what his or her actions are doing to the rest of the group. Try to gain the person's cooperation. Encourage the person to concentrate on positives, not negatives.

Participant is: Unable to express self so that everyone understands.

Participant may be: Nervous, shy, excited or not used to participating in discussions

What to do: Rephrase, restating what the person said, asking for confirmation of accuracy. Allow the person ample time to express him or herself. Help the person along without being condescending.

Participant is: Always seeking approval.
Participant may be: Looking for advice; trying to get leader to support his or her point of view; or trying to put leader on the spot.
What to do: Avoid taking sides, especially if the group will be unduly influenced by your point of view.

Participant is: Bickering with another participant.
Participant may be: Carrying on an old grudge or feeling very strongly about the issue.
What to do: Emphasise points of agreement, minimise points of disagreement. Direct participants' attention to the objectives of the meeting. Mention time limits of the meeting. Ask participants to shelve the issue for the moment.

Participant is: Too quiet, unwilling to contribute.
Participant may be: Bored, indifferent, timid, insecure; more knowledgeable or experienced than the rest of the group.
What to do: Direct questions to the person that you're quite sure s/he can respond to. Capitalise on the person's knowledge or experience by using him/her as a resource person.

Participant is: Seeking attention.
Participant may be: Feeling inferior or hiding a lack of knowledge by clowning around.
What to do: Keep reminding the person about the topic being discussed. Talk to the person privately. Point out what his or her actions are doing to the rest of the group.

Participant is: Uninvolved and unwilling to commit to new tasks.

Participant may be: Lazy; too busy already or feeling s/he should not have been asked to the meeting in the first place.

What to do: Ask for facts concerning the person's schedule. Ask the person to volunteer for tasks (others in group must as well). Make sure you ask the right people to future meetings.

Participant is: Already too over-committed to other things to take on new tasks.

Participant may be: Unaware of own skills and abilities or lacking in organisational skills.

What to do: Ask for facts concerning the person's schedule. Ask the person whether s/he is already over-committed. Tell the person you're counting on him or her. Send the person to a time-management seminar.

Participant is: A buck-passer who blames others for anything negative that happens and doesn't accept new tasks readily.

Participant may be: Unable to admit to making mistakes or afraid to take risks.

What to do: Make the person account for his or her actions. Ask for facts to back up allegations. Privately ask why the person won't accept new tasks.

CHAPTER ELEVEN

COUNSELLING INTERVIEWS

Does your problem involve unacceptable behaviour of one or more of your staff?

Why supervisors/managers hate disciplining their staff:

When asked, *"What is their most distasteful task as a supervisor,"* disciplining their staff is always high on the list. They use such excuses as:

"I hate bawling anyone out."

"Maybe the situation isn't so bad anyway."

"Hopefully their behaviour will improve without my causing a fuss."

None of these excuses work. You may ask, "I know I have to do and say something, but I don't know where to start. How can I get the results I want and make the experience easier for myself and fair to the employee I have to reprimand?"

Have a meeting with the offending employee remembering that your main goal is to improve the conduct of the employee, not to make them want to retaliate or have hurt feelings over the interview. Remind yourself that one of your major supervisory functions is to check or *"critique"* the work of those who work for you. This is different from criticising them. You'd be identifying the things they did right along with the things they did wrong. Your job is to get their best performance. To achieve this high standard of performance you must evaluate the work they've completed.

You may be tempted to let things slide, but in the future, they'll continue doing the task the *"wrong"* way, if you don't catch them the first time, they do something wrong. If you let it slide, the pattern may be locked in, which will be more difficult for the employee to change.

When critiquing work, give a summary of how they completed the task. Likely, 98 per cent of the job was done correctly, so give a summary by saying something like, *"I'm very pleased with the results of this report. The only tiny correction I'd want made is that... otherwise the rest of your performance was fine. I was impressed with the way you expressed yourself regarding the... Keep up the good work!"*

Whenever you must correct behaviour - don't say, *"You made a mistake."* Instead say, *"In the future, I'd like you to complete this assignment this way."* If you use this form of criticism, it will seldom be necessary to discipline an employee.

When an employee must be reprimanded for continued bad performance or behaviour, keep them informed at every stage, by explaining what the consequences will be should their undesirable behaviour or performance continue. Then it's the employee who chooses to misbehave, therefore they're the ones who initiate the discipline - not the supervisor or manager. When you've conducted yourself properly, you'll be able to get rid of the guilt feelings you may have because you've had to reprimand an employee. When disciplinary meetings are carried out correctly, it's the employee who carries the burden of guilt, not the supervisor.

Some employees seem to have an excuse for everything they've done wrong, and should you check things out, you'd find they were telling the truth. But there are so many errors made! The employee's late for work, with reports, and you're finding that things are rapidly getting out of hand. How should you deal with this? Keep reminding the employee that it's the results you're interested in, not his or her excuses. When delegating assignments, give deadlines and encourage the employee to meet those deadlines.

Supervisors must get work done through other people by planning, organising, staffing, directing and controlling. As a supervisor, anything you delegate to others reflects on you. If you delegate a task to Sally and she doesn't do a good job - who's to blame? Sally? No, you are! Your employees either make you look good - or make you look bad, depending on how well they do the tasks you've assigned to them. You can't pass the buck to them by saying, *"I asked Sally to do it - I guess she didn't do it right."* That's not good enough. You're still ultimately responsible for her actions as well as your own. So, if Sally doesn't do her job properly, you must talk to her and make attempts to improve her performance.

Firing probationary employees

Make sure you look carefully at the new employee's behaviour and productivity before their probationary period is over. Two weeks before their probationary period is over, review the new employee's performance. If there are any problems, call a meeting and explain his/her performance problems. If you're not yet sure, let the employee know that their probationary period is being extended (usually two to four more weeks).

Some employees simply don't fit in, and the supervisor is faced with letting them go. Many don't know if there's a difference from a legal point of view between dismissing a probationary employee and dismissing a permanent one. The main difference between a probationary and a permanent one is that the employer has much more discretion to terminate the probationary employee. Until about ten years ago, the probationary employee had no protection. The employer had the right to terminate with no notice and didn't have to give reasons for dismissal. Nor did they give the employee an opportunity of changing his/her behaviour.

Now, the law is changed in favour of the employee. Although the probationary employee still has less job security, the employer must determine carefully whether the employee is suitable for the job and must give the employee the opportunity to correct his/her behaviour or performance discrepancies. Therefore, you need to constantly check their work and behaviour during the probationary period. Waiting until the probationary period is up - is too late.

Disciplining former peers:

It's particularly difficult if the people you're now managing are your former peers. What kind of problems could occur if you were chosen as the new supervisor of several of your former workmates?

1. They may be jealous, envious, or angry.
2. Former peers may indulge in sabotaging efforts, gang up on you, or become un-cooperative.
3. They know your weaknesses and may take advantages of you.
4. They may expect favouritism from you if you're a friend or expect you to show bias towards them if they know you don't like them.
5. Will not show respect to you as their supervisor.
6. May alienate themselves from you.
7. May feel they're better qualified than you.
8. YOU may go on a power or ego trip and mismanage your responsibilities.

To alleviate this from happening, a certain set of steps should have been taken BEFORE you started in your job:

1. The supervisor/manager, who was responsible for giving you the promotion, should explain to the unsuccessful candidates why they weren't chosen for the position.
2. On the first day the supervisor takes the position, the person they report to should call a meeting with the new supervisor and his/her staff. The supervisor introduces the new supervisor to the staff, makes a statement such as, *"I expect all of you to give the same performance for our new supervisor as you did for Bill Jones who's now been promoted to another position."* The manager then leaves the room and hands over the meeting to the new supervisor.

How you continue with the meeting from this point onward is crucial to how you're ultimately accepted in the position. What would you do? Would you go over what changes you wished to make? Explain that you'll do your best to fill the position? How would you start out?

If you don't deal with the negative feelings that are there, you're lost from day one, and will probably have to put up with many negative actions from your former peers. Instead, deal with the major problem by saying, *"I know several of you applied for this position, and I can understand if you're disappointed because you weren't chosen for this position. However, our company has appointed me to this position, and to carry out my responsibilities, I'll require the same co-operation you gave Bill in the past."*

The next step is critical as well. Look at each person you're addressing, and ask, *"Mary, can I count on you to give me the same co-operation?"* Watch Mary's body language to determine whether you can expect trouble in the future. If she shrugs her shoulders, smiles and says, *"Sure,"* you're not likely to have problems with her in the future. Ask every employee the same question and observe the responses. Their body language (be it their body position, facial expressions or tone of voice) will tell you whether you can expect trouble.

Then s/he would add, *"Although I have worked with all of you, I don't really know the full function of your positions. Therefore, I will be having a meeting with each of you in the next two weeks, so I know precisely what your responsibilities are."* At those meetings the supervisor would discuss the job description of the person and ask about their career aspirations. For staff that seemed to still be upset about not getting the promotion, s/he would say, *"Is there anything I can do to make this transition easier for you?"* Then could add: *"I will do everything I can to prepare you for the next promotional opportunity."*

If the employee still balks and tries to make life miserable for you, start the disciplinary procedure to ensure that their productivity and behaviour improves. Otherwise, their negative behaviour may contaminate the rest of your staff.

Should you be socialising with your new staff? Many will say, *"Yes."* And you can, except you must impose a rule - no discussing business while socialising. However, if you socialise with only one of your staff - what are the rest of them thinking? They might be assuming that the employee you see socially will receive favouritism from you. You must weigh the pros and cons of continuing this kind of friendship. It's also important for you to realise that you now have a new peer group, and that peer group is other supervisors.

The best solution is to gradually wean yourself away from your former peer group. You're now in the position where you must discipline your former peers the same as you would any staff you supervise. Be ready psychologically to do so by placing some distance between you and your new staff.

Sometimes supervisors pick a *"pet"* employee who seems to *"get away with murder"* while another (that they can't get along with) gets blamed for trivial and unimportant things. You must always be unbiased towards every employee you supervise. Unless all the staff members are treated equally, they may think the new supervisor is treating a staff member with favouritism or is biased against them.

Differences between counselling and disciplinary interviews:

A dual approach to discipline is recommended; that of counselling and disciplinary interviews. Normally a counselling interview is enough, providing it's done soon enough, and the problem hasn't escalated beyond repair. This leaves pure disciplinary interviews for chronic or serious offences.

Interview Objectives:

See which step you forget during counselling or disciplinary interviews:

1. Clarify the problem. *"Joe, you've been late for work three times in the past two weeks - on May 4th, the 8th, and the 13th."*
2. Make sure there's agreement as to what the actual problem is. *"Do you agree that you were late those three dates?"* (In this case you should have timecards, or facts to prove they were late, in case they deny this fact.)
3. Gain the employee's participation and commitment to solving the problem. *"What do you think you can do to be on time in the future? Can I count on you to do this?"* Notice that you're concentrating on starting good behaviour (positive), rather than on stopping bad behaviour (negative).
4. Consequences should the behaviour continue. *"I'll have to place a written warning on your file if you don't correct this problem immediately."*

Interview pointers:

At any type of interview where you must discuss behaviour or need to criticise others:

1. Focus on the problem; not the employee.

2. Don't try to get the employee to admit that s/he's wrong.

3. Listen to the employee.

4. Stress that you need the employee's help

5. Don't push for an immediate solution if it's not possible.

6. Consider only those ideas suggested by the employee that are usable and appropriate.

Where should interviews be held?

The issue of *"Territory"* is important when you're dealing with discipline. A person has an *"edge"* when they're in their own territory, or on their own *"turf."* When conducting a counselling interview try to find a non-threatening an environment as possible to conduct your interviews. This would be:

First Choice: At employee's workstation (providing you can have privacy) or

Second Choice: In a conference room (providing you can have privacy) or

Last Choice: Your office (very threatening to the employee).

You want to have the edge at disciplinary interviews, so conduct these kinds of meetings:

- In your office

- If person is very timid or likely to get emotional, make the environment less threatening like a neutral territory. Your second choice could be to sit on chairs facing each other, or at a round table of some sort.

- If that's not available - at your desk, with them sitting at the side of the desk.

- If the situation is more serious, have him/her sit across the desk from you.

- If it's extremely serious (and you require a power base) have him/her sit in a chair lower than yours, or if you're of small stature (or a woman disciplining a larger man) stand up while he's sitting down.

Before explaining the method, I recommend, it's important for all readers to check out the way their companies handle discipline. If you work in a unionised environment, there may be different methods of how you're to conduct disciplinary interviews. This section is mainly for those who work in non-union or smaller companies where discipline may not have cut-and-dried policies and procedures set down on how to handle discipline.

Counselling interviews

Counselling interviews are informal interviews that deal with minor performance or behavioural problems. It's considered a verbal warning, but supervisors should document the interview in case further action is warranted. These interview notes are kept in a confidential file for the supervisor's eyes only. They do not go on the employee's personnel file because it's not a written warning. However, should the incident escalate, copies may later be attached to more formal reprimands where documentation is placed on the employee's personnel file (written warnings).

When are counselling interviews warranted?

You would use counselling interviews to deal with the following problems:

- Safety procedures aren't being followed (only if you're not sure employee knows the rules). If they know the rule is a condition of employment and break those rules, the penalty could be as severe as immediate dismissal.

- Employee shows prejudice against a peer or client.

- Production slow-down or sloppy work.

- Personality clashes.

- Abuse of work hours or coffee breaks, etc.

If done properly, counselling interviews correct minor problems. They open the door to effective communication between the employee and supervisor. It's possible that the employee didn't know their performance or behaviour was a problem, or that they're breaking a company rule or regulation. A counselling interview will enlighten these employees.

Difficult counselling interviews:

Occasionally counselling interviews can be difficult ones. A supervisor notices that an employee is snarling at other employees or observes that an employee seems lethargic, and his/her job performance is below normal. The supervisor calls the employee in for a counselling interview. When asked, *"What's the matter,"* the curt reply may be, *"It's none of your business!"*

What would you reply if you were their supervisor? You should say, *"Yes, it is. Whenever your behaviour affects your productivity or those around you, it IS my business."* Then encourage them to discuss the problem.

If they still refuse add, *"You have two choices. Give me a chance to help you with your problem or get along better with your workmates and improve your job performance (or whatever was the problem). Which have you decided to do?"*

Wait for an answer. Then, let them know that you expect their behaviour to improve and give the consequences should they not be willing to change.

What do you do if the person gives you the *"silent treatment?"* State your perception of the problem and allow the person to think about it. State your expectations but keep the door open for further discussions when the employee has cooled down. This will allow the employee to settle his/her own temper and be less emotional and angry when you decide to settle the issue.

Other personal problems may surface at this kind of interview:

- family break-up

- alcoholism

- drug abuse

- illness in the home

- problems with children

- problems with spouse

- elderly parents living with them

How would you deal with these problems? Are you qualified to handle them? In most cases - no. Therefore, supervisors should keep abreast of where people can go to obtain counselling to solve these kinds of problems. Help them obtain this help, then back off. Make allowances on the job if necessary, but eventually stick to performance issues. Remain objective. Keep emotions in check. It's difficult to think and respond to an employee's need, if you react with emotion yourself.

Keep in mind that the problem is the other person's - don't take responsibility for it. Do however try to help him/her get through the problem. When dealing with issues of this kind, confidentiality is a must! Don't discuss these issues with others unless they're critical to solving the problem.

What do you say, if an employee brings others' behaviour into the discussion?

For instance,

"Joe does that all the time - why are you picking on me?"

Your answer should be, *"We're here to discuss your performance - not Joe's."* You should then:

- State your perception of the problem and allow the person to think about it.
- State your expectations and keep the door open for further discussions when the employee has cooled down. This will allow the employee to settle his/her temper and be less emotional or angry when they decide to deal with the issue.

When you call an employee in to discuss a behaviour or production problem, keep in mind what you wish to accomplish. Let's assume that the employee requires an interview. Here's how you plan an interview, (whether it be a counselling or disciplinary interview):

Planning a counselling interview:

1. Prepare reference notes to use during the interview and keep track of pertinent facts of the case. Feel free to refer to your notes and tell the employee that you'll be taking notes during the interview. They can also take notes.
2. Make sure you have all the necessary Information required to back up your claims.
   - To deal with excessive absenteeism, you'd need attendance records.
   - For a performance problem, you'd need examples of work done or production output.
3. Plan the Sequence of the interview. Make sure you know the questions you need to ask to gain the necessary information.
4. Confirm Privacy. This is of utmost importance when conducing this type of interview. Regardless of the

nature of the problem, employees will feel far more comfortable and open if they can speak freely. Their comfort zone will lower drastically if they're worried about interruptions, and/or other people overhearing your conversation.

5. Use of hearsay information. Are you allowed to use second-hand information? What if another person said she saw Sally shopping the day she said she was away from work because of illness? Unless this employee was willing to sign a statement that she did see the person shopping, don't use this information. Instead, when you call the person in for the interview, ask, *"Why were you absent on Thursday?"*

If she says, *"I was sick,"* look them in the eye and say, *"Are you sure you were ill that day?"* Because the employee will have the suspicion that you already know they weren't away because of illness, many will confess that it was a day they wanted off for other reasons. If they don't confess, you'll have to watch subsequent absences, and if they become chronic, ask for a doctor's certificate for every illness.

On the other hand, if it was you who saw her shopping when she was supposed to be away because of illness, feel free to use the information on the interview.

6. Allow enough time to conduct interviews properly. Unexpected issues may take more time to resolve than you anticipated.

7. Decide where to hold the interview. Choose the proper environment to suit the severity of the problem.

Note: The above steps may not be possible if you're faced with having to conduct an interview spontaneously. These situations occur when:

- asked for by the employee

- you notice the employee is visibly upset

- employee broke important company rules

Conducting a counselling interview:

Until you're very comfortable in conducting this kind of interview, it's recommended that you take a list of these steps with you to the interview. Don't be afraid to refer to them. It will help you obtain the objectives of the interview and keep you on track should the employee throw a *"curve"* during the interview.

1. As you perceive it, state the performance or behaviour discrepancy or company rule being broken.
2. Ask the employee to verify that this is indeed the problem.
3. Ask the employee why the problem exists.
4. Ask the employee what affect this action will have on others in the area (if applicable). This is a powerful interviewing tool. Many don't use it because it results in a *"guilt trip"* for the employee. Use it if they appear oblivious of the affect their performance or behaviour has on others in the area.
5. Ask the employee what s/he has attempted to do so far, about the problem.
6. Ask the employee what else s/he had considered doing and what the consequences would have been?
7. Ask the employee, *"How do you think you could solve this problem?"*
8. Ask the employee, *"How can I help?"* (Optional)
9. Get the employee's commitment to the agreed upon course of action.
10. Make sure that the employee is aware of the consequences should the unacceptable behaviour or performance continue.
11. Summarise the interview by stating your perception of the problem, your expectations, and necessary guidelines.
12. Document the interview (hand written notes - do NOT put on personnel file).
13. Follow up

Documentation:

Interview notes are essential should the problem escalate, and it becomes necessary for you to conduct a more serious disciplinary interview. Follow the instructions given on how to document disciplinary interviews. This documentation does NOT go on the person's personnel file - rather they remain in your own confidential files.

Most supervisors have a confidential file, where they keep information handy for easy reference for when they do performance appraisals. This information would include special projects the employee completed, performance above and beyond the call-of-duty, problems with attendance, any counselling sessions they've had with them, etc.

Follow up:

The follow-up is very important. Along the way, you may follow-up informally. For instance: If an employee has been coming late to work, being at their workstation and saying, *"Good Morning,"* will keep tabs on the employee. At some time, however, commend them on the positive change in their behaviour.

If the problem warrants a follow-up, set an appointment to discuss the matter - usually within two weeks or a month (whatever suits the situation). Or you may wish to set this up at the time of the counselling interview. Then ask yourself:

1. Did the employee do what s/he originally planned?

2. If s/he didn't - why not?

3. If employee did do what s/he originally planned, was s/he successful?

4. If solution didn't work - why not?

5. What other suggestions can you make and follow through?

Questioning employees:

Your role in supervisory counselling consists of these three steps:

1. Helping the individual recognise the realities s/he must deal with.

2. Assisting in identifying problem areas.

3. Demonstrating your support and assistance in helping them change.

Supportive Questions:

To perform this role effectively (especially steps 2 and 3) requires frequent use of supportive questioning. These comments show acceptance and understanding of the feelings of the person we're talking to (empathy). They show your willingness to be of aid in his/her efforts to grow and change.

Examples:

1. "You feel that you're not getting co-operation from..."

2. "How can I help you get this roadblock removed?"

3. "You seem to be saying that you feel you're capable in this area."

Exploratory Questions:

These responses are made to encourage further examination of an area even though the facts may be unpleasant. The intent of these questions is to encourage mutual problem-solving.

Examples:

1. "Tell me more about that."

2. "What seems to be the difficulty here?"

3. "When did this first start?"

4. "How does this relate to your performance?"

Judgmental Questions:

These are responses of an evaluative type where we pass judgement upon what we've been listening to.

Examples:

1. "You should have done..."

2. "Have that finished by 3 o'clock."

3. "That's a good idea."

4. "That doesn't seem like much of a problem."

The judgmental response is the type most frequently used by supervisors (and usually appropriately so) when working with employees. In counselling situations, judgmental listening is not very desirable because too often it hampers open communication.

Maintaining improved performance:

If you want your employees to keep up their changed behaviour or performance, you will have a meeting and:

1. Describe the improved performance.

2. Explain the importance of this improvement to you and the employee's work group.

3. Listen empathetically to the employee's comments.

4. Ask the employee if there's anything you can do to make it easier for him/her to do the job.

5. If appropriate, tell employee how you're going to help him/her.

6. Thank the employee for the improved performance.

When no improvement is found:

1. Describe the situation and review the previous discussions.

2. Ask for reasons for the situation.

3. Listen and respond with empathy.

4. Identify what action you must take (written warning, suspension, termination) and why.

5. Agree on specific action and follow up date.

6. Show your confidence in the employee.

Under no circumstances use a *"wait and see"* attitude, because you're the ultimate one who will look bad if you don't act now.

Here are some of the more common reasons why supervisors must conduct interviews:

Absenteeism:

Many employees will go to work even with a runny nose and a fever. They refuse to take advantage of their company's sick pay policy and don't wish to take sick leave for minor ailments. They feel they may need this leave when they're very sick. Others feel that no one else can handle their job as well as they can and feel responsible for their performance. To them, it's part of the ethic of being a good worker. The supervisor should recognise the sacrifices made by this kind of worker. When that type of employee is away because of illness, s/he's usually too sick to perform any kind of work at all.

Other employees will be out for any and every minor ailment. They view sick leave as their right and want to take full advantage of the accrued leave. They demonstrate little responsibility for any required productivity. The fact that other workers may have to carry a larger workload, or that their company will suffer economically, is of little concern to them.

A large contributor to the breakdown of employee morale, is the fact that some employees get away with calling in sick, get paid for the day, and weren't the least bit ill. While it's difficult to determine completely who's truly ill and who isn't, steps can be taken that will tend to ensure that the privilege of sick leave with pay is not completely abused.

Employee absenteeism disrupts the flow of work, causes delays, and production problems. The quality of work suffers because tired employees are forced to work overtime, or the absent employee is replaced by others not as well trained.

On any normal working day, 4 to 6 per cent of all employees are usually absent from work! Does this surprise you? Because of this, supervisors must:

(a) Enforce company rules, otherwise employee will continue abusing them which encourages others to do so as well.

(b) Determine if there are absenteeism patterns.

(c) Make sure employees know that being paid while they're away sick is a privilege, not a right they have as an employee, and that this privilege can be removed at any time if it's being abused.

Overlong lunch hour:

Abuses such as washing up and preparing for the break and getting organised after the actual break, add up to a lot of extra time lost from production. In addition, the actual time off the premises or at the cafeteria seems to grow when no effort is made to monitor this abuse.

While a supervisor may close his/her eyes to the lost time as being of small consequence, the few employees who get away with the extended lunches will cause adverse effects on employee morale. It's always better not to hedge. Get to the issue - no game-playing. The supervisor should confront the person openly and tell him/her that they're abusing their lunch hour.

After lunch, the supervisor should be available to assess late employees. Several discipline possibilities exist, including docking for lateness, minimising overtime and changing the hour for lunch for some of the employees who are presenting a problem.

"Marty, I see you're still having difficulty getting back on the job at one o'clock. Starting tomorrow, let's try having your lunch hour start at twelve thirty and see if that's better."

How can one expect the other employees to be attentive to the lunch-hour time requirements when some of the employees get away with extended lunch hours?

Coffee break abuses:

Most companies allow fifteen minutes in the morning and afternoon for allotted coffee breaks. Studies indicate that some sort of break in the work schedule increases production. Some firms permit their employees to have their coffee and snacks at their workstations or desks. No time is set for the break, and it tends to fit into the normal flow of work. Any congregating is discouraged. Many employees don't want to interrupt their flow of work, either because they use the slacker moments for the snack or because they may not care to have something to eat.

The second type is a work stopping time where everyone congregates in one area, be it a lunchroom or cafeteria. Supervisors must discourage employees from slowing down in anticipation of the coffee break. At the conclusion of the break, the resumption of work must be commenced otherwise the fifteen-minute coffee break can extend by five minutes beforehand and then five minutes afterward (bathroom break). The management personnel could be visible immediately before and after the coffee break. They can make direct observation of abuses and encourage more productive use of time. Handing out assignments, checking on progress and other supervisory functions can be accomplished prior to, and right after the break.

Despite efforts, some employees will look upon the coffee break as an opportunity to socialise and waste time. Only the conscientious effort on the part of the management personnel to observe abuses and restrict excessive break activity will cause the segregation of those who occasionally abuse, from those who will consistently abuse the time allotted.

Smoke Break Abuses:

The length of smoke breaks must comply with the company's allotted coffee and lunch break times. Most companies now have implemented *"no smoking"* laws on their premises, and many buildings do not allow smoking on the premises. Therefore, smokers are forced to smoke outside the buildings where they work. In some cases that too is illegal so smokers sometimes must go great distances to be able to smoke.

However, they must abide by their company's ruling regarding coffee and work break timelines.

CHAPTER TWELVE
DISCIPLINARY INTERVIEWS

Preparing yourself psychologically:

As a supervisor/manager you'll face many disciplinary problems. If I anticipate an interview being a difficult one, I rehearse the situation with a colleague of mine. The colleague plays *"Devil's Advocate"* and is as difficult as he can be. In our role-playing, I'm able to try out different approaches until I find one that will work best. Then when the actual interview takes place, I'm not faced with unexpected problems.

The discipline procedure:

Here are the normal steps taken in the disciplinary procedure. Problem situations may not have all these steps. For instance: If the situation is serious enough, step 4 may be the only step taken (Always check your union agreement first before considering the following):

1. Verbal warning and counselling interview.

2. First written warning and disciplinary interview.

3. Second written warning and disciplinary interview (optional).

4. Dismissal, termination, or firing (whichever term your company uses).

Disciplinary interviews:

Before conducting a disciplinary interview, be sure to prepare for it. Questions you might ask yourself are:

When should the interview take place?

If you must terminate an employee, when would you choose to do so?

Most managers would agree that the discipline often must happen when the infraction occurs. In other situations, you may not have to act immediately. If that's done, choose the latter part of the day, when the employee can go home and think about the situation. If they have further work to do, it may change their concentration level, or they may not produce the normal work expected of them. Termination of an employee would follow the same course. At times, the employee can be fired on the spot if the situation is serious enough.

Conducting a disciplinary interview:

Take the following steps if you've preceded the disciplinary interview with a counselling interview:

1. Summarise what has taken place using any documentation that you've made before the interview.
2. Ask the employee why in his/her opinion s/he hasn't resolved the problem. Remain flexible - new information may warrant further counselling.
3. Ask the employee if there's any further information or suggestions s/he might have. Once again, this is a decision making-point - you may decide to try the counselling approach once more considering new information.
4. Set authoritative guidelines. For example: *"Tomorrow, you must start coming in on time. We've given you every opportunity to solve your problem. If it's not solved by then, I'll have to take further action (specify)."*
5. Get the employee's agreement that s/he understands your position. Ask the employee, *"What is your understanding of the situation?"*
6. Attempt to get his/her commitment to determine a course of action which will solve the problem. Ask a question such as, *"Are you willing to try to meet my expectations?"* Be supportive, *"I know you can do it."*
7. Be sure that the employee is aware of the consequences should the unacceptable behaviour or performance continue.
8. Document the interview.
9. Follow up within a reasonable length of time.

If this is the first interview, leave out the steps relating to counselling interviews.

Documentation:

Disciplinary interviews are tougher to conduct than counselling interviews because written warnings must be put on the employee's file. Take care that this documentation is accurate.

Normally, three copies are made, one for the employee, one for the manager, and one for the employee's personnel file. If the employee was terminated, they might decide to start legal action and charge you and your company with wrongful dismissal. In that case, your documentation would be used in a court of law - so do it correctly!

It's important to check to see what your company normally does to document interviews. It's possible that they don't include enough information on their documentation to win a case in court.

Purpose of Documentation:

- Provides a permanent record that the interview took place.

- Provides an accurate statement should it need to go to a higher authority in the company, or to a court of law.

- Serves as an indicator to an employee that the matter under discussion is a serious one.

- Provides an agreement for follow up purposes at an agreed upon date.

Suggested content:

Employee's name
Employee's number
Employee's position
Manager's name
Manager's title
Unit or branch
Location
Date and time of interview

Place of Interview

Who at interview?

Purpose of interview

Information given by manager

Questions asked by the manager

Answers and additional information given by employee

Effect the employee's action had on others

Course of action agreed upon

Consequences should problem persist (discipline)

Follow up interview date and time

Signature of employee

Signature of manager

Signature of union representative (if required)

Signature of any witnesses

Note: These are suggested headings - use whatever appears applicable to the situation.

Who should type this report, or should it be hand-written? Preferably you will prepare them on your computer and store them in a confidential file. If you don't have access to a computer, your Human Resources or Employee Relations department staff (who deal every day with confidential information) would be able to prepare these reports. If you hand print the information, make sure you use black pen because blue ink does not copy as well. Make sure all information stays confidential.

If the employee refuses to sign the document, insert the comments *"Employee refused to sign document."* Then give date and either initial or sign in full.

It's important to emphasise that, in documenting the inter-view, you record the facts of the situation not assumptions, inferences or your feelings about it! Make your notes right after the conclusion of the interview.

How long do you think written warnings should remain on an employee's personnel file? Your company probably has a set time. If it doesn't, evaluate each situation individually. If the employee has had no other problems for a year, I'd probably remove the warning from their file. Most employees feel as if a cloud is hanging over them if warnings are on their file. Many use tunnel vision, when performing their duties and stop taking any kind of risk. Some lower their productivity level.

On the other hand, if the employee has been in several *"scrapes"* in the past year, leave warnings on his/her file. A pattern is showing here that may lead to more serious discipline and possibly termination.

If an employee asked to see his/her personnel file, would you show it to them? By law you have to make it available to them within twenty-four hours. This should remind you not to put anything on their personnel file that would appear as if you were discriminating against them. If viewed by the employee, they may take your interview notes describing them as biased, stereotyped or prejudiced. Clean out all employee personnel files to remove this possibility. Don't neglect follow-up interviews which are much more important in the case of disciplinary than counselling interviews. Set a date at the time of the initial interview.

Reasons for this are:

1. If people are doing what they're supposed to be doing, the manager should recognise that achievement and act accordingly.
2. If not, the manager must offer additional assistance or take further disciplinary action.

Types of disciplinary action:

Before deciding which kind of disciplinary action you wish to take, check to see what the normal procedures are in your company or industry are. Also check union agreements and employee manuals to see what options might be identified for infractions.

A. Written warning with consequences of further action, possibly termination

B. Suspension from work with pay

C. Suspension from work without pay

D. Demotion - be careful of this one. In many areas it's considered that if you demote an employee, you've first (unofficially) fired them and have re-hired them at a lower-level position. This would make it necessary for you to have very accurate documentation as to why you *"fired"* them.

E. Transfer to another job or area

F. No promotion until behaviour warrants it

G. Termination or dismissal

Exit Interviews:

These are meetings set up when an employee decides to leave your company voluntarily. Their input about problems they encountered can be a key to help you to keep your department running properly. Unfortunately, many employees worry about what kind of reference you'll give them, so play it safe, and keep quiet about things you really need to know. This information may enable employers to cut down drastically on employee turnover.

If a pattern starts to appear in a department, higher management should ask themselves whether it may be because of the manager or department head in the area and ask pertinent questions of staff leaving the company.

When conducting exit interviews, it's important to ask open-ended questions. Let the employee know that you want to learn everything they have to say about the job they're leaving - both positive and negative. Ask them to be very honest with you so the company can overcome any reason they might have left that they perceive as being the company's fault.

CONCLUSION

I hope this book will help you problem-solve and make decisions with the following issues relating to:

* Business
* Personal issues
* Manpower planning
* Time wasters
* Resistance to change
* Conflict resolution
* Training of staff
* Training of supervisors
* Career development
* Listening
* Meetings
* Counselling interviews
* Disciplinary interviews

We also discussed:

*Brainstorming
*The importance of planning
*The lack of job descriptions
*Setting standards of performance
*Visualisation
*Rehearsals
*Supervisors from Hell
*Personality types
*Introvert/Extrovert
*Sensory Language
*Cultural and personality differences

*Chairing a meeting

*Problem participants at meetings

*Difference between counselling and disciplinary interviews

*Documenting interviews

*Maintaining improvement of performance

*Exit interviews

You might also wish to purchase Roberta Cava's other business oriented books such as:

Dealing with Difficult People

Dealing with Difficult Situations – at Work and at Home

Dealing with Workplace Bullying

What am I going to do with the rest of my life?

Interpersonal Communication at Work

Change? Not me!

How Women can advance in business

Survival Skills for Supervisors and Managers

Human Resources at its Best!

Human Resources Policies and Procedures - Australia

Employee Handbook

Easy Come – Hard to go – The Art of Hiring, Disciplining and Firing Employees

Time and Stress – Today's silent killers

www.ingramcontent.com/pod-product-compliance
Lightning Source LLC
Chambersburg PA
CBHW050505210326
41521CB00011B/2326